Patterns *for* Prayer

Volume: January – April

ALVIN VANDERGRIEND

Love2Pray

PRAYERSHOP PUBLISHING

Terre Haute, Indiana

PrayerShop Publishing is the publishing arm of the Church Prayer Leaders Network. The Church Prayer Leaders Network exists to equip and inspire local churches and their prayer leaders in their desire to disciple their people in prayer and to become a "house of prayer for all nations." Its online store, prayershop.org, has more than 150 prayer resources available for purchase or download.

ISBN (Print): 978-1-970176-13-1

ISBN (E-Book): 978-1-970176-14-8

Original contributors to this prayer guide include Edith Bajema, Dian Ginter, Joan Huyser-Honig, Don McCrory, Laurie Quist, Al Schaap, Mark Timmer, Alvin J. VanderGriend, and Jean Westenbroek.

TABLE OF CONTENTS

PREFACE

This book is designed to help you develop a meaningful and disciplined personal prayer life. I have heard people say, "I'd like to pray more, but after five minutes I run out of things to pray about." Most of us know what that's like. *Patterns for Prayer* is for all who have "run out of things to pray about."

Regular use of this prayer guide will help you

- learn to use the language of Scripture in prayer
- use all of the elements of prayer regularly
- claim the promises of God with confidence
- keep your thoughts from wandering during prayer
- pray expressively for friends and family
- release God's power and grace for your church and the kingdom of God
- develop the habit of praying for unsaved friends and acquaintances

You'll discover a weekly cycle in these pages as you pray for the leadership and ministries of your own local church. You'll pray about worship, church leaders, outreach ministries, church education, world missions, caregiving and fellowship, and financial stewardship.

This guide is meant to enlarge and deepen your prayer life. It is not intended to be the whole of it. Let these prayer suggestions trigger prayer expressions from your own heart. Where they do not fit, customize them to your own situation. Space is provided on each page for you to keep a record of further petitions and intercessions.

The Heidelberg Catechism reminds us that "God gives his grace and Holy Spirit only to those who pray continually and groan inwardly, asking God for these gifts and thanking him for them" (Q&A 116). I pray that you may do just that and, in so doing, find that your life is enriched as you grow in intimacy with God and receive a generous amount of his grace and Spirit.

—Alvin J. VanderGriend

JANUARY 1

Personal Prayer

Praise God for his creativity. Give glory for the unending variety exhibited in his creation. Thank God for the wonderful way you have been made and for your unique personality, gifts, and talents. Confess any dissatisfaction you have had with the way you have been created. Commit yourself to serving God with your gifts and talents. Ask that God may reveal your spiritual gifts to you and give you opportunity to use them for him.

For Your Family and Friends

Pray that family members and friends will be a source of joy and blessing to each other and that together they may experience the joy and blessing of the Lord.

For the Church

Pray that pastors may speak the Word of God with power and conviction so that God's people may hear the Word and do it, be equipped for discipling, and witness boldly to the good news.

For the Kingdom

Pray that the gospel may reach, touch, and renew the hearts and minds of people without hope in our world today so that there may be a great harvest of souls brought into the church.

For the Unsaved

Since "no one can come to [Christ] unless the Father . . . draws him" (Jn. 6:44), pray that God will draw your unsaved relatives, friends, and acquaintances (it's best to name them) to himself.

JANUARY 2

Personal Prayer

Praise the prayer-hearing God that his ear is attentive to your prayers. Give thanks for the privilege of coming into God's presence and conversing with him through prayer. Confess any personal failure in your prayer life that you are aware of. Commit yourself to being a faithful intercessor. Ask that God will strengthen your prayer life and help you to pray in the Spirit with all kinds of prayer, on all occasions, for all God's people (Eph. 6:18).

For Your Family and Friends

Pray for unity in the Spirit. Ask for a deep love for, and understanding between family members and friends, and for reconciliation where they are at odds.

For the Church

Pray that your church's leaders—pastors, elders, deacons, and others—may be filled with the Spirit and be effective in the ministries to which they are called.

For the Kingdom

Pray that the leaders of your denomination will clearly discern God's will and vision for your churches. Ask that they will use their spiritual gifts to lead the church in that direction.

For the Unsaved

"The harvest is plentiful but the workers are few. Ask the Lord of the harvest, therefore, to send out workers into his harvest field" (Mt. 9:37-38). Pray that God will send helpful believers (this could be you) to unsaved persons you care about.

JANUARY 3

Personal Prayer

Praise God for his matchless grace. Give thanks that his grace is sufficient for you in every situation. Confess any do-it-yourself efforts in which you have rejected God's grace and tried to go it alone. Commit yourself to being a channel of that grace to others. Ask that God will meet your needs according to his glorious riches in Christ Jesus (Phil. 4:19) and that his grace will be poured out abundantly.

For Your Family and Friends

Pray for the salvation of each family member. Ask that children may come to trust Christ at an early age and may desire to become part of God's forever family.

For the Church

Pray for each of your church's outreach ministries, for the leaders, and for those being reached, that God will use all these efforts to bring people to himself.

For the Kingdom

Lift up the names of the leaders of your nation, state/province, and community, asking that the Lord's strength and wisdom come to full maturity in each one as they learn to rely on him.

For the Unsaved

Pray that the unsaved persons you name before God may seek him, reach out for him, and find him, since he is not far from each one of us (Acts 17:27).

Prayer Pointer

"Our business in prayer is not to prescribe, but to subscribe to the wisdom and will of God; to refer our case to him, and then leave it with him." —Anonymous

JANUARY 4

Personal Prayer

Praise God for his limitless power. Give thanks that God is willing to strengthen you with power through the Spirit within you. Confess any time that you have been weak because you did not avail yourself of his strength. Commit yourself to serving in the strength of the Lord. Ask that out of his glorious riches God will strengthen you with power through his Spirit in your inner being (Eph. 3:16).

For Your Family and Friends

Pray that your family and/or friends will experience rich times of praying together, playing together, and worshiping together.

For the Church

Pray for your church's teachers and counselors that they may communicate Bible truths clearly, live holy lives before God, and be Christ-like examples to those they lead.

For the Kingdom

Pray for small group Bible studies as they meet weekly in homes and churches all across the continent. Ask God to change hearts and lives through the Word.

For the Unsaved

Pray that unsaved persons you know may receive the free gift of God, which is eternal life, and may not have to receive the wages of sin eternally (Rom. 6:23).

Prayer Pointer

"When you pray, rather let your heart be without words than your words without heart." —JOHN BUNYAN

JANUARY 5

Personal Prayer

Praise God for his unswerving faithfulness in keeping all his promises and never forsaking his own. Give thanks that God gave his only begotten Son that whoever believes in him should have everlasting life. Confess any unfaithfulness on your part to God. Commit yourself to being faithful to all your loved ones and to keeping all the promises you have made to them. Ask God to fill you with the Holy Spirit and to give you the confidence that you are a member of his family and know God as "Abba Father."

For Your Family and Friends

Support family members and friends in their work or studies and pray that each may be diligent in pursuit of God-given tasks.

For the Church

Pray for your church's missionaries (by name, if possible), asking the Lord to encourage and strengthen them and to keep them from loneliness, discouragement, spiritual attack, and burnout.

For the Kingdom

Pray for your denomination's world mission efforts as missionaries are recruited, trained, sent out, and supported. Pray for adequate funds to carry on and expand the work.

For the Unsaved

Pray that unsaved persons who hear the Word of God will receive it and accept it not as the word of human beings, but as it truly is, the Word of God (1 Thess. 2:13).

JANUARY 6

Personal Prayer

Praise God for his unfathomable love. Give thanks that he will let nothing separate you from that love. Confess to God any lack of love for him. Commit yourself to loving the Lord with all your heart, soul, mind, and strength. Ask that your love may grow and overflow to others just as Christ's love does to you (1 Thess. 3:12).

For Your Family and Friends

Pray for family members and friends to have a strong and growing love for God and for others.

For the Church

Pray for your church's caregivers that they may be gems of Christ's love and compassion and may be his hands and feet to reach out to many human needs today.

For the Kingdom

Pray that God will bless the efforts of relief ministries throughout the world as they help the church to motivate and empower members for works of mercy so that hurts are healed and needs met.

For the Unsaved

Pray that the Holy Spirit will convict unsaved persons you know (again, be specific), bringing them to repentance and faith and guiding them into all truth.

Prayer Pointer

"I have lived to thank God that all my prayers have not been answered." — Jean Ingelow

JANUARY 7

Personal Prayer

Praise Jesus Christ for his incomprehensible humility. Thank him for humbling himself to die on the cross that you might be set free. Confess any pride, egotism, or boastfulness you find in yourself. Commit yourself to doing nothing out of selfish ambition or vain conceit, but in humility considering others better than yourself (Phil. 2:3). Pray that you may have the mind of Christ in all matters such as priorities, goals, time management, vocational choices, relationships, and recreation.

For Your Family and Friends

Pray about weaknesses you see in family members and friends, asking specifically that God may overcome each weakness by his strength.

For the Church

Ask that God's people will give generously and cheerfully, according to the blessings they have received, that the financial needs of your church will be adequately met.

For the Kingdom

Pray for the church throughout the world that its divisions may be healed, its leaders endowed with the Spirit's power, its people filled with zeal for the cause of Christ, so that the church may increase daily and the kingdom be advanced.

For the Unsaved

Pray that the Holy Spirit may give you a burden for lost people like that of the apostle Paul, who expressed "great sorrow and unceasing anguish in [his] heart" over lost people (Rom. 9:1-3).

JANUARY 8

Personal Prayer

Praise God for his inexhaustible goodness. There is nothing lacking or defective in him. Give thanks for all the pleasure and blessings which flow from God's goodness. Confess any ingratitude to him. Commit yourself to God-like goodness. Ask that today you may grow in the grace and knowledge of the Lord Jesus Christ (2 Pet. 3:18).

For Your Family and Friends

Pray that your children will grow up in the training and instruction of the Lord and will learn to walk in his ways (Eph. 6:4).

For the Church

Pray that all who proclaim the gospel today may be clothed with power from the Holy Spirit (Acts 1:8) and may preach the Word of God boldly and clearly. Ask that worshipers may have open ears and attentive hearts, and that they may experience God's presence.

For the Kingdom

Pray for the unreached people groups worldwide to be reached with the gospel. Ask for laborers, open doors, adequate funds, and a positive response.

For the Unsaved

Pray that those who seek the Lord will seek him with all their heart and will find him (Deut. 4:29).

Prayer Pointer

"When you go to your knees, God will help you stand up to anything."
—ANONYMOUS

JANUARY 9

Personal Prayer

Praise God that he knows everything in every age. Give thanks that he knows you by name and that you matter to him. Confess any attempt to conceal things from God. Commit yourself to openness and honesty before God. Invite him to search your heart and life (Ps. 139:23-24). Ask to be protected from the evil one and kept from a spirit of worldliness.

For Your Family and Friends

Pray that each family member and friend may be responsive to God's grace and may live a life pleasing to him.

For the Church

Pray that your church leaders may grow in grace, in knowledge, and in wisdom as they continue in the Word of God and prayer.

For the Kingdom

More than 100,000 persons are added each day to the church worldwide. Pray for new converts that they may stand firm in the faith and may grow spiritually strong.

For the Unsaved

Since faith comes by hearing, and hearing by the Word of God (Rom. 10:15-17), pray that your unsaved friends, neighbors, and relatives will hear the Word and respond in faith.

JANUARY 10

Personal Prayer

Praise God for the depth of his wisdom and knowledge, and for his unsearchable judgments. Thank God for guiding and directing your ways. Confess any resistance on your part to do his will. Commit yourself to acknowledging him in all your ways (Prov. 3:5-6). Ask God for the Spirit of wisdom and revelation, so that you may know him better and have the eyes of your heart enlightened, to know the hope to which you are called, the riches of his glorious inheritance (Eph. 1:17-18).

For Your Family and Friends

Pray that by God's grace, parents will be able to train their children in the ways of the Lord and that their children will always walk in these ways (Prov. 22:6).

For the Church

Pray for the Spirit of love in your church that believers may be one, even as the Father and Son are one, so that the world may believe that God sent Jesus Christ (Jn. 17:21).

For the Kingdom

Pray that measures honoring the sanctity of life will become law in the U.S. and Canada.

For the Unsaved

Pray that the Holy Spirit, who is sent to convict the world of guilt in regard to sin, righteousness, and judgment (Jn. 16:8), will work powerfully and effectively in the hearts and lives of unsaved persons you name.

JANUARY 11

Personal Prayer

Praise God for keeping his covenant promises to you. Give thanks that you have always been able to count on him in all circumstances. Confess any doubt you have had concerning God and his promises. Commit yourself to trusting the Lord and taking him at his word. Ask for his peace which transcends understanding to guard your heart and your mind in Jesus Christ.

For Your Family and Friends

Pray that family or personal financial problems may be eased and that each person may become a good steward of God-given financial resources.

For the Church

Pray that those who instruct within the church may be able to correctly handle the Word of truth (2 Tim. 2:15).

For the Kingdom

Pray for those who work in denominational publications that they may produce the educational material that will give strength to the church's educational ministries, lead many to Christ, and help all to be built up in the faith.

For the Unsaved

Name specific unsaved persons and pray that they may "repent and be baptized . . . in the name of Jesus Christ for the forgiveness of [their] sins. And [that they] will receive the gift of the Holy Spirit" (Acts 2:38).

Prayer Pointer

"Embark upon no enterprise you cannot submit to the test of prayer." — Anonymous

JANUARY 12

Personal Prayer

Praise God for the beauty of his holiness (2 Chron. 20:21). Give thanks that he has removed the stain of sin from your life and made you holy. Confess any sin or unholiness that taints your life. Commit yourself to being holy, as God is holy (1 Pet. 1:16). Ask that you may be made holy through and through so that your spirit, soul, and body will be kept blameless (1 Thess. 5:23).

For Your Family and Friends

Pray for families undergoing severe marital strife, asking that God will rekindle a flame of love between husband and wife.

For the Church

Pray that God will give your church a vision for the mission task so that all will be motivated to pray and give faithfully.

For the Kingdom

Pray that laws against pornography will be enforced and new and more effective laws will be passed in Canada and the U.S. Pray for decency and morality in our countries.

For the Unsaved

Jesus said, "Whoever hears my word and believes him who sent me has eternal life" (Jn. 5:24). Pray that unsaved friends, neighbors, and associates will hear, believe, and be saved.

Prayer Pointer

"God eagerly awaits the chance to bless the person whose heart is turned toward him." —Anonymous

JANUARY 13

Personal Prayer

Praise Jesus Christ for his grace and beauty. Thank God for reproducing the beauty of Christ's character in you. Confess anything in your life which is displeasing to God. Commit yourself to pleasing him in every way. Ask God to help you live a life worthy of the Lord, to please him in everything you do, and to bear fruit in every good work (Col. 1:10).

For Your Family and Friends

Pray that each one of your family members and friends will develop a close personal relationship with the Lord and spend regular quiet times with him.

For the Church

Pray that members of your church will lovingly bear one another's burdens and so fulfill the law of Christ (Gal. 6:2).

For the Kingdom

Pray that all God's people will be able to stand against the principalities, powers, and the world rulers of darkness that seek to control the lives and destinies of people. Pray that they may put on the whole armor of God and may pray in the Spirit with all kinds of prayers and requests (Eph. 6:10-18).

For the Unsaved

God "commands all people everywhere to repent" (Acts 17:30). Pray that unsaved persons you know will come to the end of human efforts and excuses, and will turn away from sin unto God.

JANUARY 14

Personal Prayer

Praise the Lamb who is worthy "to receive power and wealth and wisdom and strength and honor and glory and praise" (Rev. 5:12). Thank God for the blood of the Lamb given for the complete remission of all your sin. Confess any self-centeredness which has taken your focus off God. Commit yourself to loving God with all your heart and soul and mind and strength, and your neighbor as yourself. Ask him to give you the kingdom and make you his priest that you may serve him and reign with him on earth.

For Your Family and Friends

Pray that sons and daughters who have wandered away from the faith may be restored.

For the Church

Pray that God will free you from the love of money and keep you from making it a god, showing you how to be content with what you have and how to lay up treasures in heaven.

For the Kingdom

Pray for your nation and its leaders that they may be enabled to rule according to God's good pleasure, to the hindrance of wickedness so that all may lead quiet and peaceable lives.

For the Unsaved

"Everyone who calls on the name of the Lord will be saved" (Acts 2:21). Pray that unsaved persons you know may call on the name of the Lord and be saved.

JANUARY 15

Personal Prayer

Praise God as your rock, your fortress, your deliverer, the one in whom you take refuge. Thank God that he hears and answers prayer and showers you with unfailing kindness. Confess any unfaithfulness, impurity, or deceit. Commit yourself to courageously challenging the Lord's enemies as you are armed by his strength. Ask him to reach down and take hold of you, to arm you with strength, and to rescue you from evil powers.

For Your Family and Friends

Pray that family members and friends will be sensitive to the needs of others around them and will have a desire to help and care for them.

For the Church

Pray that your pastor will be used of the Lord to equip the saints for the work of ministry that your church may be built up. Pray that visitors to your worship services may be noticed, receive a warm welcome, and find worship meaningful.

For the Kingdom

Pray for agencies which assist established churches and newly planted churches to gather God's growing family. Pray for adequate funds, excellent resources, and effective leaders.

For the Unsaved

Pray that God will lay a burden on your heart for one or more unsaved persons he wants you to reach out to. He does not want anyone to perish (2 Pet. 3:9).

JANUARY 16

Personal Prayer

Praise the one who is King of kings and Lord of lords. Give thanks for everything in which you may find godly pleasure today: for work, food, books, music, and friends. Confess any pain you have unnecessarily brought into the lives of others. Commit yourself to doing to others today what you would have them do to you. Ask God to guide you in all your ways, to guard you against all that would harm you in body and soul, and to strengthen you in the face of temptation.

For Your Family and Friends

Pray that family members and friends will be protected from any temptation, such as sexual sin, love of money, desire for power, or overeating.

For the Church

Pray for your deacons, elders, and pastor. Ask God to give them wisdom and integrity and the filling of the Holy Spirit, that they may be mature in faith and may exercise their offices with prayer, patience, and humility.

For the Kingdom

Pray that officials in your city, state/ province, and nation will make decisions in accord with biblical justice and morality.

For the Unsaved

Pray that the seed of the gospel sown in the hearts of unbelievers may find good soil and produce a crop to the glory of God (Mt. 13:4-8).

JANUARY 17

Personal Prayer

Praise God as your beloved Father. Give thanks as a dear child for the undeserved love and grace you receive from him. Confess all the ways you have offended him. Commit yourself to trusting and obeying. Ask Christ to be with you always and to teach you to obey all things that he has commanded.

For Your Family and Friends

Pray for the ability to serve God in marriage and family life by reflecting his covenant love in lifelong loyalty, and by teaching his ways, so that children may know Jesus as their Lord and learn to use their gifts in a life of joyful service.

For the Church

Pray that your church may engage in and promote the work of evangelism so that those who are still sheep without a shepherd will experience your care, feel your love, and hear the good news through you.

For the Kingdom

Pray that God may help you be a good earthkeeper and caretaker, loving your neighbor, tending the creation, and using your skills in the unfolding and well-being of his world.

For the Unsaved

Pray that the Lord may open the hearts of unsaved persons to respond to the good news (Acts 16:14).

Prayer Pointer

"God's answers are wiser than our prayers." —ANONYMOUS

JANUARY 18

Personal Prayer

Praise the one who is able to do immeasurably more than all one can ask or imagine. Thank God for what he is doing in your life and in the church in response to prayer. Confess little asking and weak praying. Commit yourself to asking and expecting much in Jesus' name. Claim the promise that Christ will come to you and make his home in your heart if you love him and trust him.

For Your Family and Friends

Pray that your family may grow closer as children grow older and prepare to leave home. Ask the Lord to keep family and friendship ties strong and full of love across distances which separate.

For the Church

Pray for leaders, teachers, and committee personnel, that they may be qualified for and committed to their ministries. Ask that their ministries may make a difference in the lives of those they lead.

For the Kingdom

Pray that the countries currently banning the Bible may soon rescind these bans so that their people may have free access to the Bible.

For the Unsaved

God "commands all people everywhere to repent" (Acts 17:30). Pray specifically for unsaved persons you know, that they may repent and believe as God commands.

Prayer Pointer

"Prayer should be the key of the day and the lock of the night." —Thomas Fuller

JANUARY 19

Personal Prayer

Praise him who is able to keep you from falling and to present you faultless before his presence with exceeding joy. Give thanks that God has preserved you through many physical and spiritual dangers. Confess a specific fault that you want God to remove. Commit yourself to courageous endurance in the way of Christ. Ask for undying hope in the Lord and a renewal of strength that you may soar on wings like an eagle, may run and not grow weary, may walk and not be faint (Isa. 40:31).

For Your Family and Friends

Pray that family members and friends of dating age may be wise in their dating choices and may be kept pure and spotless in their relationships. Ask God to give wisdom to each one in selecting a life partner.

For the Church

Ask the Lord to send the power of his Holy Spirit upon all the missionaries of your church and to give them the strength, courage, health, support, and spiritual gifts to be fruitful.

For the Kingdom

Pray that Christian colleges, Bible schools, and seminaries may effectively integrate the Christian faith into their curriculums as they prepare young men and women to serve as godly leaders.

For the Unsaved

Pray for specific unsaved persons that they may confess with their mouths, "Jesus is Lord" and believe in their hearts that God raised him from the dead (Rom. 10:9) and be saved.

JANUARY 20

Personal Prayer

Praise the righteous God whose face shines upon you (Psalm 4). Thank him for setting apart the godly for himself. Confess any unresolved anger that causes you to sin. Commit yourself to bringing to God gifts worthy of his name. Ask the Lord to surround you with his favor and spread his protection over you so that you may rejoice in him.

For Your Family and Friends

Pray that children may accept wise spiritual guidance from their parents and from spiritual mentors in the church.

For the Church

Pray that God will send holy angels to protect this flock from the attacks of Satan and his demons. Ask him to give your people supernatural strength to resist temptation.

For the Kingdom

Pray that the Spirit may thrust believers into worldwide mission, impelling young and old, men and women, to go next door and far away, into science and art, media and marketplace with the good news of God's grace.

For the Unsaved

Pray that by the power of the Holy Spirit unbelievers may "draw near to God with a sincere heart in full assurance of faith" (Heb. 10:22) so their hearts may be sprinkled and their guilty consciences cleansed.

JANUARY 21

Personal Prayer

God is light; in him there is no darkness at all. Praise God for the radiance of his presence. Give thanks that you can have fellowship with him and walk in the light. Confess any dark sin that you have not yet exposed to that light. Commit yourself to living by the light of God's truth (1 Jn. 1:5-7). Ask "that your love may abound more and more in knowledge and depth of insight, so that you may be able to discern what is best and may be pure and blameless until the day of Christ, filled with the fruit of righteousness . . ." (Phil. 1:9-11).

For Your Family and Friends

Pray for husbands that they will give spiritual leadership in their households and will love their wives as Christ loved the church.

For the Church

Pray that your church family may be so in love with the Lord, so wanting to please him, that they will see giving as a privilege and a joy, and will make tithing a way of life.

For the Kingdom

Pray that the kingdom of God will spread measurably, visibly, and irresistibly in all parts of the world. Ask that the kingdom of Satan be destroyed.

For the Unsaved

Pray that unsaved persons will receive "Christ Jesus as Lord, continue to live in him, rooted and built up in him, strengthened in faith . . . and overflowing with thankfulness" (Col. 2:6-7).

JANUARY 22

Personal Prayer

Magnify the Lord and exalt his name. Give thanks for the privilege of corporate worship. Confess any irreverent use of his name or wrong use of his day. Commit yourself to worshiping in Spirit and truth. Ask for the fruit of the Spirit in your life: love, joy, peace, patience, kindness, goodness, faithfulness, gentleness, and self-control (Gal. 5:22-23).

For Your Family and Friends

Pray for wives who will have the God-honoring beauty described in 1 Peter 3, who will love their husbands as the church loves Christ, and who will develop their gifts and skills for the sake of family and kingdom.

For the Church

Ask that believers' hearts may be prepared to hear from God and that pastors may faithfully proclaim the Word of God and relate it well to the needs of listeners. Pray that in worship God will receive the glory and the congregation will be edified.

For the Kingdom

Pray that the Lord of nations will bring peace and tranquility in this war-torn world as more and more believers unite in prayer for national renewal, spiritual awakening in the church, and the extension of God's kingdom worldwide.

For the Unsaved

Pray for specific unsaved persons that they may "want to know Christ and the power of his resurrection and the fellowship of sharing in his sufferings, becoming like him in his death, and so . . . attain to the resurrection from the dead" (Phil. 3:10-11).

JANUARY 23

Personal Prayer

Praise God, who is your refuge and strength (Psalm 46). Give thanks for his "ever present help in trouble" (v. 1). Confess any desire to live life apart from God. Commit yourself to being still and knowing that he is God. Ask him to prosper you and not harm you, to give you hope and a future (Jer. 29:11).

For Your Family and Friends

Pray that children and young people will choose godly companions and be protected from those who would lead them astray or wrongly influence their thinking.

For the Church

Pray that your pastor may have a fruitful ministry and that he may handle responsibilities with grace and patience. Ask that he may have a harmonious working relationship with other congregational leaders.

For the Kingdom

Pray for governments to do public justice and to protect the freedoms and rights of individuals, groups, and institutions.

For the Unsaved

Pray that you may "let your light shine before men, that they may see your good deeds and praise your Father in heaven" (Mt. 5:16). Offer to be used of God to reach certain individuals.

Prayer Pointer

"Prayer is the most vital force in world evangelism." —Anonymous

JANUARY 24

Personal Prayer

Praise God as the blessed and only Ruler over all things (1 Tim. 6:15). Thank him for sustaining all things by his powerful Word and holding all things together. Confess any situation in which you have resisted God's rule in your life. Commit yourself to knowing and doing his will. Ask the Lord to put a hedge of protection around you and your loved ones.

For Your Family and Friends

Pray that the lives of children will be filled with growing love, true knowledge, and mature judgment so they will be able to choose what is best (Phil. 1:9-10).

For the Church

Pray that God will give your church members opportunities to witness to people and invite them to church (Col. 4:2-4).

For the Kingdom

Pray for nominal Christians who are caught in worldliness, lukewarmness, ignorance, indifference, and fruitlessness in their religious lives (2 Tim. 3:2-5). Pray that they may be awakened to the true realities of the Christian faith.

For the Unsaved

Pray that unsaved friends, relatives, and neighbors may come to know that "salvation is found in no one else [than Christ], for there is no other name under heaven given to men by which we must be saved" (Acts 4:12).

JANUARY 25

Personal Prayer

Praise God that he is absolutely holy; that there is no sin in him at all. Thank him for making you holy through the blood of Jesus Christ. Confess any known sin that is contrary to God's will. Commit to his lordship in every area of life. Ask that in all you are facing, your faithful God will "not let you be tempted beyond what you can bear," but will always "provide a way out so that you can stand up under it" (1 Cor. 10:13).

For Your Family and Friends

Pray that families and friends experiencing financial problems will be strengthened in faith as they look to God for their "daily bread." Pray that they will seek his blessing and guidance in vocational and financial choices.

For the Church

Pray that children and young people of your church will commit their lives to Jesus Christ, make public profession of faith, and become fruitful members of the kingdom.

For the Kingdom

Pray for Christian schools and colleges, for wise board members, for supportive parents, and godly teachers. Ask God to help the church fulfill its duty of caring for and nurturing its children.

For the Unsaved

Pray that your Christian example may encourage others to seek the Lord. Ask that you will "always be prepared to give an answer to everyone who asks you to give the reason for the hope that you have" (1 Pet. 3:15).

JANUARY 26

Personal Prayer

Praise God that he is trustworthy. Give thanks that his unfailing love surrounds all who trust in him (Ps. 32:10). Confess any doubt you find in your heart. Commit yourself to knowing God better. Ask him to reveal himself to you through his Word and Spirit in the midst of life's circumstances.

For Your Family and Friends

Pray for parents who will create homes that are safe havens for the children, places where love is both tender and tough.

For the Church

Pray that your missionaries will have God's guidance regarding how to present the gospel in a different culture. Ask that they will know God's priorities in order to make the best use of their time.

For the Kingdom

Pray for laborers to be called into God's harvest field. Ask that hearts may be prepared to accept the gospel, and that the necessary tools, such as Bibles and Christian literature, may be readily available.

For the Unsaved

Pray that the barriers to salvation faced by unbelievers today may be demolished, that many may come into the kingdom.

Prayer Pointer

"Who rises from prayer a better man, his prayer is answered." —George Meredith

JANUARY 27

Personal Prayer

Express your love and admiration for the Father, the Son, and the Holy Spirit. Thank the Father for his love, Christ for his grace, and the Holy Spirit for his fellowship. Confess any unresponsiveness to the Father's love, the Savior's grace, and the Holy Spirit's inner working. Commit yourself to loving God with all your heart, soul, mind, and strength. Ask that you may become a temple of the living God so that he will live in you, walk with you, and be your God (2 Cor. 6:16).

For Your Family and Friends

Pray that each family member and friend may develop a close walk with God and spend time with him each day to nurture this relationship.

For the Church

Pray for a congregation whose members are bound by love to each other and willing to say "I am sorry; please forgive me." Pray that the Spirit may mold your congregation into a loving, redemptive fellowship.

For the Kingdom

Pray for those in law enforcement that they may be recognized as God's servants working for the good of the community, "hold[ing] no terror for those who do right, but for those who do wrong" (Rom. 13:3).

For the Unsaved

Pray that the unsaved may realize that life is meaningless apart from God. Ask that they will seek true meaning in him.

JANUARY 28

Personal Prayer

Praise God as the only true God who has revealed himself to you in his Word and through his Son. Give thanks for the Bible through which God reveals himself and his will for your life. Confess any failure to use and respond to that revealed Word. Commit yourself to meditating on the Word and allowing it to dwell richly in your heart (Col. 3:16). Ask that you may remain in Christ and his words in you, so that you can bear much fruit to the Father's glory (Jn. 15:7).

For Your Family and Friends

Pray that children may respect and obey their parents, and that parents may bring up their children in the training and instruction of the Lord (Eph. 6:4).

For the Church

Ask God to supply wisdom to those in charge of your congregational budgets so that dollars received in offerings will be wisely distributed in ways which recognize the Lord's priorities.

For the Kingdom

Pray that the church will be empowered to tell the good news to a world where millions are estranged from God. Ask that believers everywhere will proclaim the forgiveness of sins and new life for all who repent and believe.

For the Unsaved

Pray by name for unsaved friends and neighbors that they may know the love of God, may believe in his Son Jesus Christ, and will not perish but have everlasting life (Jn. 3:16).

JANUARY 29

Personal Prayer

Praise God for the depth of his love, which is the very core of his being (1 Jn. 4:8-9). Thank God that he will never take his love from you or your family (Ps. 103:17). Confess any times during the last week when you gave little thought to God's great love for you. Commit yourself to beginning each day with the refreshment of God's love (Ps. 90:14). Ask that you "may have power . . . to grasp how wide and long and high and deep is the love of Christ, and to know this love that surpasses knowledge" (Eph. 3:17-19).

For Your Family and Friends

Pray that their experience of God's love through you will change their lives.

For the Church

Ask that visitors to your church will sense the love of God in your fellowship and be drawn to find more of it in God's family.

For the Kingdom

Pray for specific places in the world where violence, greed, and hatred are wounding many lives. Pray that this work of Satan will be defeated, overpowered by the love of God shown through Jesus and his church.

For the Unsaved

Pray that the unsaved persons you know will come to know God's love by hearing about the sacrifice of his only Son (1 Jn. 4:10).

JANUARY 30

Personal Prayer

Praise God as the source of every thing that is good, holy, just, and beautiful. Thank God for inviting you to remain in him, as a branch remains in the vine, so that you too can produce fruit that is good and holy (Jn. 15:7-8). Confess your failure to "remain in" Jesus, to find your fullness and your satisfaction in him. Be specific about the things that crowd out your desire to abide in him. Commit yourself to finding your fullness in Jesus during this day. Ask him to show you that apart from him you can do nothing (15:5).

For Your Family and Friends

Pray that parents will be so firmly rooted in Jesus that their children cannot miss seeing the fruit that they bear as his disciples.

For the Church

Pray that the spiritual leaders of your church will see their need to be abiding daily in Jesus and his Word, constantly in prayer, and completely dependent on him for their ministry.

For the Kingdom

Pray that Christians in positions of leadership—business, politics, medicine, teaching—may remain firmly attached to Christ and so bring glory to his name.

For the Unsaved

Make a list of the unsaved persons you know, and ask God to graft each one into the tree of life (Rom. 11:17).

Prayer Pointer

"Arguments never settle things, but prayer changes things."—ANONYMOUS

JANUARY 31

Personal Prayer

Praise God for his deep compassion for the poor, the suffering, the lonely (Isa. 58:5-7). Give thanks for the times when God has lifted you out of the pit of depression or loneliness or from the mire of circumstances (Ps. 40:2). Confess any times recently when your ears have been deaf to the cries of the poor in your area (Mt. 25:31-46). Commit yourself to becoming more aware of their needs. Ask God to show you his heart of compassion and how it can be revealed in your life (Isaiah 58).

For Your Family and Friends

Pray that those friends who are struggling with problems will receive from you the compassion and encouragement they need to go on.

For the Church

Pray that those involved in outreach ministries will offer comfort, compassion, and understanding for those who suffer from poverty, loneliness, abuse, guilt, and insecurity (2 Cor. 1:4).

For the Kingdom

Pray that oppressive governments may learn to respect the rights of all people and that true justice and mercy will prevail in courts and government decisions.

For the Unsaved

Pray that the unsaved persons on your list may experience God's love and compassion through the Christians they meet today.

FEBRUARY 1

Personal Prayer

Praise God that "from him and through him and to him are all things" (Rom. 11:36). Thank God for being both your dwelling place and your destination. Confess times that you have tried to live independently of his authority. Commit yourself to offering your body "as [a] living sacrifice, holy and pleasing to God" (Rom. 12:1). Ask God to help you in "whatever you do, whether in word or deed, [to] do it all in the name of the Lord Jesus" (Col. 3:17).

For Your Family and Friends

Pray for children who struggle against authority, especially adolescents and teens, that they may find God's authority to be good and right in their lives.

For the Church

Pray for teachers who teach with both word and deed how to wholeheartedly love and serve the living God.

For the Kingdom

Pray for your local and regional public officials, that they may remain free from corruption and resist the temptation to misuse their authority.

For the Unsaved

Pray for all the unsaved persons in your city, that "at the name of Jesus every knee should bow, . . . and every tongue confess that Jesus Christ is Lord" (Phil. 2:10-11).

Prayer Pointer

"Prayer is hardest when it is hardest to pray."—Anonymous

FEBRUARY 2

Personal Prayer

Praise God, "the blessed and only Ruler, the King of kings and Lord of lords, who alone is immortal and who lives in unapproachable light" (1 Tim. 6:15-16). Thank him for being the light of the world. Confess any areas of your life that you may have been ashamed to bring into the light of God's truth. Commit yourself to living as a child of the light. Ask God to fill you with the fruit of light: all goodness, righteousness, and truth (Eph. 5:9).

For Your Family and Friends

Pray that any situations of family abuse may be brought into the light and healed.

For the Church

Pray that the missionaries your church supports may be like shining stars in dark places as they hold out the word of life (Phil. 2:15-16).

For the Kingdom

Pray along with thousands of other believers that God will send spiritual renewal to your country and community, pushing back apathy and materialism and setting hearts on fire for the gospel.

For the Unsaved

Pray that those who are sleeping in the darkness of their sins will wake and rise from their sleep of death, that Christ may shine upon them. Pray also that, as God's light in this world, you may make the most of every opportunity (Eph. 5:14-16).

FEBRUARY 3

Personal Prayer

Give glory to God as the Lord of peace. Thank Jesus that he himself is our peace, breaking down the barriers and the dividing walls of hostility (Eph. 2:14). Confess any areas where you are not at peace with another believer or group of Christians. Commit yourself to making every effort to live in peace with all people (Heb. 12:14). Ask God to help you bear with others and forgive whatever grievance you have against them, forgiving them as the Lord forgave you (Col. 3:13).

For Your Family and Friends

Pray for God's peace to be restored between husbands and wives where there is conflict and lack of forgiveness.

For the Church

Pray that the church may "make every effort to keep the unity of the Spirit through the bond of peace" (Eph. 4:3), realizing that as members of one body we are called to peace.

For the Kingdom

Pray for those who are called to settle disputes in our society—labor arbitrators, family counselors, court-appointed mediators, judges, juries—that they may discern the truth and restore goodwill and peace.

For the Unsaved

Pray that the restlessness and conflict in their lives will drive them to seek the peace of God, which transcends all understanding (Phil. 4:7).

FEBRUARY 4

Personal Prayer

Praise God as the giver of every good and perfect gift (Jas. 1:5, 17). Give thanks for the indescribable gift of his only Son. Confess any times when you have taken God's gifts to you for granted. Commit yourself to searching Scripture for more knowledge of the "riches of God's grace that he lavished on us" (Eph. 1:7-8). Ask that your heart's thirst be quenched and your soul's hunger be satisfied in God as with the richest of foods (Psalm 63).

For Your Family and Friends

Pray that their private and family devotions be filled with thanksgiving, and that their hearts be moved to give to causes that help a needy world.

For the Church

Pray that your congregation may have faith that "you will be made rich in every way so that you can be generous on every occasion" (2 Cor. 9:11).

For the Kingdom

Pray for the agencies that show God's love to the needy in your community, that they not only may supply needs but also bring in overflowing expressions of thanks to God (9:12).

For the Unsaved

Pray that they might accept the gospel and be able to say, "How great is the love the Father has lavished on us, that we should be called children of God!" (1 Jn. 3:1).

FEBRUARY 5

Personal Prayer

Praise the King for his powerful rule in this world, and that no plan of his can be thwarted (Job 42:2). Give thanks that this rule is evidenced around us and in us. Confess any doubts which you may have about God's kingly power. Commit yourself to being a living sacrifice, holy and pleasing, as your spiritual worship to God (Rom. 12:1). Ask that you would "never be lacking in zeal, but keep your spiritual fervor, serving the Lord" (12:11).

For Your Family and Friends

Pray that unconditional love will be demonstrated clearly and consistently in your family relationships and friendships. Ask the Lord to give you a fuller appreciation for those whom he has placed in your life.

For the Church

Pray that, as worshipers gather this week, they will be eager to exalt the Lord for his goodness and that their worship will move them to greater obedience.

For the Kingdom

Pray that, in a world filled with sin, "justice will roll on like a river, righteousness like a never-failing stream" (Amos 5:24).

For the Unsaved

Pray that unsaved persons whom you know will ask the reason for the hope that you have, and that you may be prepared to give an answer (1 Pet. 3:15).

Prayer Pointer

"Prayer is an end to isolation. It is living our daily life with someone; with him who alone can deliver us from solitude." —Georges LeFevre

FEBRUARY 6

Personal Prayer

Praise the saving God whose paths are beyond tracing out! (Rom. 11:33). Give thanks for his continual, personal care for you. Confess any failure to maintain a healthy relationship with the Lord. Commit yourself to disciplined, joyful Christian living, recognizing the tremendous blessing of belonging to Jesus Christ. Ask that you will be "joyful in hope, patient in affliction, faithful in prayer" (Rom. 12:12).

For Your Family and Friends

Pray that children will respect their parents as the God-given authority in their lives, and that the counsel of senior family members and friends will be honored.

For the Church

Pray that church leaders will resist Satan's schemes and will use their influence to lead the church to fulfill its mission of making disciples.

For the Kingdom

Pray that world leaders will have compassion and wisdom and the courage to lead. Ask God to work in the hearts of these men and women, that they might see him as their strength.

For the Unsaved

Pray that any personal difficulties experienced by unsaved persons around you may be opportunities for them to come to know the grace that is found in Jesus Christ.

FEBRUARY 7

Personal Prayer

Praise the heavenly Father, who has become your Father through Jesus Christ. Give thanks that in Jesus Christ you have been given a heavenly citizenship. Confess those habits which draw you from his love. Commit yourself to finding all that you desire in the Lord. Ask to be delivered from the power of the evil one.

For Your Family and Friends

Pray that family members and friends will reflect the lordship of Christ in their daily schedules, and that relationships will not be neglected.

For the Church

Pray that outreach will receive top priority in all the ministries of the church. Ask God to give his people a renewed vision to carry on the strategic mission of the church.

For the Kingdom

Pray that people who are gripped by the power of money may be freed. Ask God to show these individuals the value of heavenly treasure.

For the Unsaved

Jesus came, not for the healthy, but for the sick. Pray that unsaved persons whom you know will receive spiritual health by faith in Jesus Christ.

Prayer Pointer

"The right way to pray, then, is any way that allows us to communicate with God. For prayer is not a ritual; it is the soul's inherent response to a relationship with a loving Father." —Colleen Townsend Evans

FEBRUARY 8

Personal Prayer

Praise the God who cares even for the birds (Mt. 6:25-34). Give thanks that you can depend upon him completely to meet every need. Confess anything in your life which is rooted in pride and self-reliance. Commit yourself to not worrying about your life or about tomorrow. Ask the Father to help you to "seek first his kingdom and his righteousness . . ." (6:33).

For Your Family and Friends

Ask the compassionate Lord to remember single parents and their children.

For the Church

Pray that the truth will impress the people of your church in a way that causes them to be disciples who disciple others. Ask that words and lives will tell about Jesus.

For the Kingdom

Pray that the judges of the land will be ones who love justice and mercy.

For the Unsaved

Ask that unsaved persons around you will realize the folly of building their lives on foundations of sand. Pray that they will build on the rock, Jesus Christ.

FEBRUARY 9

Personal Prayer

Praise the Maker of heaven and earth for the marvels of creation in this world. Thank the Lord that he never slumbers or sleeps and that he constantly watches over you. Confess those times in which you refuse God's help and resent his watching over you. Commit yourself to trusting fully in the Maker of heaven and earth. Ask that God himself will make you strong, firm, and steadfast (1 Pet. 4:13).

For Your Family and Friends

Pray that marriages in danger of breaking up will be healed and the pain of divorce avoided.

For the Church

Ask God to show churches how they can help to take the gospel to all nations. Pray that these churches will be motivated to do their part.

For the Kingdom

Ask God to encourage and support people whom you know with physical and mental limitations.

For the Unsaved

Pray that God will lead you to befriend an unsaved person. Ask God to use this relationship to bring that new friend to Jesus.

Prayer Pointer

"The first purpose of prayer is to know God."—Charles L. Allen

FEBRUARY 10

Personal Prayer

Praise God that Jesus Christ is coming again to bring all things to perfection. Thank the Lord that you can anticipate dwelling with him in a new heaven and earth. Confess any attitudes or actions which are hindering the coming kingdom. Commit yourself to watching and praying, being ready for the coming of Christ. Ask that you may live in a way pleasing to God, so that he might say to you, "Well done, good and faithful servant" (Mt 25:21).

For Your Family and Friends

Pray that your family and friends will submit to one another out of reverence for Christ (Eph. 5:21).

For the Church

Ask God to make his people generous in giving their time and gifts for the benefit of others. Ask that the love of Christ will be evident in the care Christians give to each other.

For the Kingdom

Pray that those who suffer the effects of mental illness will find appropriate care. Remember also the families of these individuals.

For the Unsaved

Pray that the unsaved will see that "all have sinned and fall short of the glory of God" (Rom. 3:23), and find their justification in Christ.

FEBRUARY 11

Personal Prayer

Praise God that he is completely trustworthy and that he has never failed anyone (Jn. 14:1-23). Thank God that Jesus Christ is preparing a place for you at this very moment. Confess any reluctance to trust God in everything. Commit yourself to living with your heart as Christ's home. Ask the Lord to do great things through you in the power of the ascended Lord.

For Your Family and Friends

Pray that you and your family and friends will not be ashamed of the gospel, which is God's power for salvation (Rom. 1:16).

For the Church

Pray that church members will view their finances as belonging to God and will give as the Lord has given to them.

For the Kingdom

Ask that our society will respect the value of human life at every stage of life. Pray especially for people who today are making decisions about the life of another.

For the Unsaved

Jesus said, "I am the way and the truth and the life. No one comes to the Father except through me" (Jn. 14:6). Pray that unsaved persons whom you know will accept this truth.

Prayer Pointer

"Trouble and perplexity drive me to prayer and prayer drives away perplexity and trouble." —Philippe Melanchthon

FEBRUARY 12

Personal Prayer

Praise God, the giver of wisdom and power (Dan. 2:20). Give thanks for opportunities to worship with others, to learn from God's wisdom, and to be touched by his presence. Confess attempts to survive through mere human wisdom and power. Commit yourself to carefully applying what God teaches you today. Ask God to empower you to live accordingly.

For Your Family and Friends

Pray that your household and friends will be ready to learn from God's wisdom and to be touched by his power.

For the Church

Pray that God's powerful presence will be sensed from the opening moments of worship this Sunday. Ask that all will be empowered to leave with the knowledge that God can work through their lives.

For the Kingdom

Pray that your company, culture, city, and country will submit to the wisdom of God. Ask God to help you to live openly for Jesus in every area of influence.

For the Unsaved

Pray for unsaved persons you know by name. Ask God to work through the power of his Holy Spirit to convict them of sin and lead them into his truth (Jn. 16:7-11). Ask God to use you to love them.

FEBRUARY 13

Personal Prayer

Praise God, the changer of times and seasons (Dan. 2:21), who is in control of all of history. Give thanks for this new day. Confess any misuse or waste of time. Commit yourself to taking hold of today's opportunities and to enjoying the special pleasures God provides during this season. Ask him to guide you to make wise and efficient use of your time.

For Your Family and Friends

Pray that God will give you wisdom to spend time with family and friends. Ask him to protect those special times together so that your relationships will flourish.

For the Church

Pray that your church leaders will be protected from overloaded schedules. Ask God to give them wisdom as they lead the church and care for their other concerns.

For the Kingdom

Pray that local and denominational leaders will sense God's timing in deciding when to move forward with new ministries or to make changes in existing ones.

For the Unsaved

Ask God to show an unsaved friend that "now is the time of God's favor, now is the day of salvation" (2 Cor. 6:2). Pray that he or she responds to God soon, while there is time.

Prayer Pointer

"When we say to people, 'I will pray for you,' we make a very important commitment. The sad thing is that this remark often remains nothing but a well-meant expression of concern." —Henri Nouwen

FEBRUARY 14

Personal Prayer

Praise God as the one who sets up leaders and deposes them (Dan. 2:21). Give thanks for your own opportunities to lead others. Confess any negligence or cowardice in leadership. Commit yourself to being a leader of integrity wherever God gives you influence. Ask God to grant you wisdom as you influence your children, friends, employees, and others.

For Your Family and Friends

Pray for God-honoring pacesetters among the peer groups of your children. Pray that your own influence on your family and friends will lead them closer to God.

For the Church

Pray that your church's outreach efforts will be guided by a clear vision of what God can do to gather and guide his family. Pray that you will have the courage to help your church minister to people beyond the church walls.

For the Kingdom

Pray for "all those in authority, that we may live peaceful and quiet lives in all godliness and holiness" (1 Tim. 2:2). Pray that leaders who uphold God's principles will be brought to power throughout the world so that the gospel will be unhindered.

For the Unsaved

Pray that God will use you to lead someone into a right relationship with him.

FEBRUARY 15

Personal Prayer

Praise God because "he gives wisdom to the wise and knowledge to the discerning. He reveals deep and hidden things" (Dan. 2:21-22). Thank God for revealing himself to you in his written Word. Confess any lack of interest or discipline in regularly reading and meditating on God's Word. Commit yourself to a steady and balanced spiritual diet. Ask God to be your teacher, leading you to knowledge and wisdom.

For Your Family and Friends

Pray that your family and friends will grow not only in knowing about God but also in knowing God himself.

For the Church

Pray that the people who conduct your church's education ministry will diligently prepare lessons and lovingly involve themselves with their class members. Pray that both adults and children will continue to learn and grow.

For the Kingdom

Thank God for the people writing and editing church education materials. Ask that these materials will be tools to help believers apply God's Word to daily decisions.

For the Unsaved

Pray that God will use you to lead unsaved people out of the darkness of ignorance and rebellion into the light of his truth.

Prayer Pointer

"The prime need of the church is not men of money nor men of brains, but men of prayer."—E. M. Bounds

FEBRUARY 16

Personal Prayer

Praise the most high God, whose kingdom is eternal and who is sovereign over all the earth (Dan. 4:2-3, 17). Thank God for being your Lord, as well as your Savior. Confess any pockets of resistance to his rule in your life. Commit your full and lifelong allegiance to the Lord. Ask him to use you in extending his rule.

For Your Family and Friends

Pray that your family will be God's loyal subjects in his kingdom. Pray that "the footprints that we leave will lead them to believe, and the lives we live inspire them to obey."

For the Church

Ask God to develop a global vision in you and your church. Pray specifically for missionaries and their families whom you know.

For the Kingdom

Thank God for those who are called to serve as missionaries in other countries. Ask him to help them learn the languages and customs and to serve effectively as his ambassadors in lands foreign to them.

For the Unsaved

Pray that people in other countries who hear the message of the gospel presented by strangers will be led into an intimate love of God.

FEBRUARY 17

Personal Prayer

Praise God, the one who rescues and saves (Dan. 4:27). Give thanks for specific ways he is caring for you right now. Confess any areas in which you are worrying instead of praying and accepting his loving care (Phil. 4:6-7). Commit a concern to God, thanking him for his care for you. Ask him to help you believe in his willingness to handle it.

For Your Family and Friends

Pray that your family and friends may be rooted and established in love and may have "power, together with all the saints, to grasp how wide and long and high and deep is the love of Christ, and to know this love that surpasses knowledge—that [they] may be filled to the measure of all the fullness of God" (Eph. 3:18-19).

For the Church

Pray that your church will be a fellowship which experiences the signs and wonders of God's loving care. Pray for those especially in need of care or friendship right now, and offer yourself to God as his caregiving child.

For the Kingdom

Pray for relief workers extending care in the name of Jesus Christ to those suffering from recent disasters. Pray that the care is given openly in Jesus' name.

For the Unsaved

Pray for at least three unsaved people you know. Ask God to use you in finding and enfolding them into his growing family.

FEBRUARY 18

Personal Prayer

Praise God, the ultimate owner of all, who gives and takes away the privilege of managing those resources (Daniel 4). Thank God for specific resources he has put under your care. Confess any attempts to own (rather than manage) "your" money. Commit yourself to being a faithful steward who puts God's kingdom and righteousness first (Mt. 6:33). Ask him to teach you the secret of being content in any and every situation (Phil. 4:12).

For Your Family and Friends

Pray that God will give you, your family, and your friends the daily provisions you need (Mt. 6:11). Ask also that you all will excel in the grace of giving (2 Cor. 8:7).

For the Church

Pray that believers will be diligent and loving in returning the first portion of their income to God. Ask that needed church resources will be provided and handled with utmost integrity.

For the Kingdom

Pray that God's name will be honored in Christian ministries by their prudent management of resources.

For the Unsaved

Pray that the unsaved will notice the generous and enthusiastic support of gospel ministries throughout the world by God's people and be attracted to him.

FEBRUARY 19

Personal Prayer

Praise God for his holiness and righteousness. Thank him for promising to work all things together for good. Confess any coldness of heart. Commit yourself to becoming more and more conformed to the image of Christ (Rom. 8:29). Ask God to renew your love for him as it was when you first believed.

For Your Family and Friends

Pray that the future spouses of your children and unmarried friends may be persons who are godly, humble, and obedient to God. Ask God to honor himself in these marriages.

For the Church

Pray for your pastor and family today. Ask that God would use your pastor to convey his message to the church with power and anointing. Pray that your church will respond positively to the pulpit ministry with heartfelt praise and worship of God.

For the Kingdom

Lift up oppressed peoples who are open to the gospel. Ask God to prepare their hearts, to keep them from false religions, and to cause them to discern and reject false doctrine.

For the Unsaved

Ask God to lay on your heart those for whom he desires you to pray. Request the Holy Spirit to show you how to pray for each person.

Prayer Pointer

"Productive prayer requires earnestness, not eloquence." —ANONYMOUS

FEBRUARY 20

Personal Prayer

Praise Jesus for being "the same yesterday and today and forever" (Heb. 13:8). Thank him for always being with you regardless of your circumstances. Confess your weakness and inability to escape certain temptations. Commit your way to the Lord's total control. Ask for his help today to overcome sin in your life.

For Your Family and Friends

Ask the Lord to give harmony and peace to your family and friends. Pray that each person will respect and honor others, following God's plan for relationships in the family (Eph. 5:22-6:4).

For the Church

Pray that church leaders will be conscientious, seeking God's will and not their own. Ask that they will have a servant's heart in ministry and work in harmony and unity with all.

For the Kingdom

Pray that believers will be strengthened to recognize God's voice and reject the enemy's lies and tricks "in order that Satan may not outwit us" (2 Cor. 2:11).

For the Unsaved

Ask God to disturb the hearts of the unsaved so they find no rest or satisfaction in anything apart from him (Eccl. 1:2; 2:17). Pray that the Holy Spirit will bring strong conviction of sin to them.

FEBRUARY 21

Personal Prayer

Praise God for his limitless power. Thank the Spirit for being "in you" and for being "greater than the one who is in the world" (1 Jn. 4:4). Confess moments when you have limited God's power because of doubts or unbelief. Commit yourself to living in the presence and power of God every day. Ask him to make you more aware of his presence and protection daily and not to take it for granted.

For Your Family and Friends

Ask God to help children choose their friends wisely. Pray that young people will not give into the "evil desires" of this world (2 Tim. 2:22).

For the Church

Pray that each member of your church will have a strong burden for unsaved people they know. Ask that they will have the courage to speak when God gives them the opportunities.

For the Kingdom

Pray that believers worldwide will be strengthened for the spiritual battles they face. Ask that they will "put on the full armor of God so that [they] can take [their] stand against the devil's schemes" (Eph. 6:10-18).

For the Unsaved

Ask God to provide answers for unsaved persons you know who have serious questions about the claims of Christ. Pray that God will use you to provide some answers.

FEBRUARY 22

Personal Prayer

Praise God for his abundant mercy. Thank him for not punishing you as your sins have deserved (Ezra 9:13). Confess any secret sins which hold you back from full fellowship with God. Commit yourself to turning away from sin by the power of the Holy Spirit and living completely for God's glory. Ask God to restore the joy of his salvation and to grant you a willing spirit (Ps. 51:12).

For Your Family and Friends

Ask that your family and friends will hunger and thirst for God, walk closely with him always, and take time for prayer and Bible reading.

For the Church

Ask God to inspire teachers and group leaders as they prepare Bible lessons this week. Pray that they will be able to communicate clearly and faithfully.

For the Kingdom

Pray for your elected and appointed public servants. Ask that they will initiate and enact laws based on godly principles (Prov. 14:34).

For the Unsaved

Ask the Lord to create a hunger and thirst for him and his Word in the lives of unsaved persons you know. Pray that you will be sensitive to their struggles and questions.

FEBRUARY 23

Personal Prayer

Rejoice in God's majesty, glory, and might. Thank God that in all things he works for the good of those who love him (Rom. 8:28). Confess any fear, worry, or anxiety you may be feeling about your present circumstances. Commit your day to God and rest in his good planning for your life (Prov. 3:5-6). Ask for his peace to remain with you throughout your day.

For Your Family and Friends

Ask God to convict and bring back any family member or friend who has strayed from him.

For the Church

Ask God to help each member see the fields that are ready for harvest and to respond accordingly. Pray for the physical, emotional, and spiritual health of all the missionaries your church supports.

For the Kingdom

Pray that believers everywhere will walk in truth and unity. Ask the Holy Spirit to draw them closer to each other.

For the Unsaved

Pray that the Holy Spirit will show self-righteous people the truth and comfort of salvation by grace alone (Eph. 2:8-9).

Prayer Pointer

"I have been driven many times to my knees by the overwhelming conviction that I had nowhere else to go."—Abraham Lincoln

FEBRUARY 24

Personal Prayer

Praise God for his controlling presence everywhere. Give thanks that no circumstance in life—even death itself—is beyond his loving control. Confess your desire to act according to your own timetable rather than God's. Commit yourself to drawing closer to God in every way and waiting patiently for him. Ask for the ability to live by faith and not by sight (2 Cor. 5:7).

For Your Family and Friends

Request that a hedge of protection be placed around each family member and friend to fend off the enemy's attacks.

For the Church

Ask that members will have the humility and gentleness to consider others better than themselves. Pray that believers will not only look out for their own interests, but also for the interests of others (Phil. 2:3-4).

For the Kingdom

Ask God to bless the training of Christian workers who desire to take the gospel into cultures which are unlike their own. Pray that the Spirit will remove any doubt or fear from them and their families as they prepare to serve as mission workers.

For the Unsaved

Name the name of one unsaved person whom you know. Ask God to bring that person to salvation. Pray that you may be used to lead that person to Jesus and then commit yourself to obedience.

FEBRUARY 25

Personal Prayer

Praise God for caring intimately about you. Thank God for choosing you to help fulfill his plans. Confess any self-centeredness or preoccupation with your desires and needs rather than those of God and others. Commit yourself to walking under the Spirit's control, trusting him with the circumstances of life (Ps. 31:15). Ask for more sensitivity to the needs of others.

For Your Family and Friends

Ask God to meet the needs of family members and friends who are experiencing a financial, physical, or emotional crisis.

For the Church

Pray for the prosperity of the members of your congregation. Pray especially for those on fixed incomes that they will have sufficient means to live. Ask God's blessing on the deacons of your church as they manage the temporal resources of your congregation.

For the Kingdom

Ask for urgency and boldness for believers worldwide. Pray that they will never grow deaf to God's call to the harvest fields.

For the Unsaved

Pray for persons who have decided to follow false religions. Ask God to open their hearts and minds to Jesus Christ, who is the way, the truth, and the life (Jn. 14:6).

Prayer Pointer

"We ought not to tolerate for a minute the ghastly and grievous thought that God will not answer prayer. History, as manifested in Christ Jesus, demands it."
—Charles H. Spurgeon

FEBRUARY 26

Personal Prayer

Praise God as the one who can wash every part of your life clean from the stain of sin. Thank him for offering his only Son as a sacrifice for you (Jn. 3:16). Confess those times when you have listened to Satan's accusations of guilt even after confessing your sin to God. Commit yourself to receiving God's forgiveness and acceptance of you with a free and joyful heart. Ask the Lord to help you see yourself through his eyes—clean, holy, and dearly loved (Eph. 1:3-8).

For Your Family and Friends

Pray that those in your circle of relatives or friends who have not yet found cleansing for their sin may do so this year.

For the Church

Pray that the spirit of worship in your congregation is not hindered by some members' refusal to forgive others or themselves (Eph. 4:32).

For the Kingdom

Pray that those involved in fighting, racial conflict, or persecution may find God's forgiveness and cleansing and offer it to their enemies.

For the Unsaved

Pray that your love and forgiveness for your critics and opponents will attract them to the same God that you love and serve (Lk. 6:27-29, 35-36).

FEBRUARY 27

Personal Prayer

Give praise to God as the Spirit of wisdom and understanding, the Spirit of counsel and of knowledge (Isa. 11:2). Thank God for freely giving wisdom to all who ask and who trust him to answer (Jas. 1:5). Confess those times in the past week or month when you have relied on human wisdom rather than seeking God's wisdom. Commit yourself to seeking God's wisdom at all costs (Prov. 2:1-6). Ask God to show you how his wisdom is different from the world's (Jas. 3:13-18).

For Your Family and Friends

Pray that God will give your young people the discernment and ability to choose the way of wisdom over foolishness (Prov. 2:12-15).

For the Church

Pray that your church's leaders will be filled with wisdom as they make both public and private decisions, so that their whole lives will glorify God.

For the Kingdom

Pray for wisdom for all political leaders whose decisions will affect the lives of thousands or millions.

For the Unsaved

Pray that God will use you to share with an unsaved friend "the Scriptures which are able to make you wise for salvation" (2 Tim. 3:15).

Prayer Pointer

"Prayer requires more of the heart than of the tongue." —Adam Clarke

FEBRUARY 28

Personal Prayer

Worship God with reverence and awe as a consuming fire blazing with holiness (Heb. 12:28-29). Give thanks for his plan to refine your faith through trials and tests (Jas. 1:2-4). Confess any times this week when you have not seen God's purpose for you in these trials (Mal. 3:2-4). Commit yourself to submitting to God's testing in your life. Ask God to strengthen you with his power (Eph. 6:10-11).

For Your Family and Friends

Pray for those who are undergoing severe testing, that God may show them his purpose and strengthen them in their weakness (Heb. 12:7-13).

For the Church

Pray for those who work in your church's outreach programs, that they may help unsaved people to see God's love and purposes through the trials they face in their lives.

For the Kingdom

Pray that Christians in leadership positions around the world will not fall under testing but be strengthened. Their witness is crucial!

For the Unsaved

Pray that God will lead you to pray this week with an unsaved person who struggles with trials in his or her life.

MARCH 1

Personal Prayer

Praise God as the creator of all life, including your own (Isa. 45:18). Give thanks for his splendor, seen in all his mighty creation (Psalm 148). Confess to God those times when you have forgotten that all of your life and this world is a creation of God. Commit yourself to seeing your life as God's workmanship, created in Christ Jesus (Eph. 2:10). Ask God to show you the good works that he has prepared in advance for you to do.

For Your Family and Friends

Pray that parents will raise their children as the handiwork of God and encourage their children's creativity as image-bearers of the Creator.

For the Church

Pray that those who educate in the church will be able to teach children that they have a new self, which is being renewed in knowledge in the image of their Creator (Col. 3:10).

For the Kingdom

Pray for the public and private schools in your area, that they may nurture rather than stunt children's awareness of God, the Creator.

For the Unsaved

Pray that people may once again worship and serve the Creator rather than the things that God created (Rom. 1:25).

Prayer Pointer

"Teach us to pray that we may cause
The enemy to flee,
That we his evil power may bind,
His prisoners to free."—Watchman Nee

MARCH 2

Personal Prayer

Glorify the Almighty God, who has the power to defeat your accuser and deceiver, Satan (Rev. 12:7-10). Thank God that his immeasurable power is at work within you (Eph. 3:20). Confess those times when you have tried to battle against Satan in your own strength. Commit yourself to living in God's all-surpassing power (2 Cor. 4:7). Ask God to help you see how his power can be made perfect in your weakness (2 Cor. 12:9).

For Your Family and Friends

Pray that Christian families may be given the power to withstand Satan's attacks on their homes and relationships.

For the Church

Pray for your foreign missionaries, that they may be given divine power to demolish arguments and take people's thoughts captive for Christ (2 Cor. 10:4-5).

For the Kingdom

Pray for those countries that are clearly under Satan's power, marked by cruelty, injustice, and horrible poverty. Ask God to bring his light into the darkness.

For the Unsaved

Pray that, through you, Jesus might turn people from the power of Satan to God (Acts 26:18).

MARCH 3

Personal Prayer

Praise God, whose kindness toward you will last forever and ever. Thank God for loving you with an everlasting love and drawing you with lovingkindness (Jer. 31:3). Confess any ways in which you have not reflected that kindness to others. Commit yourself to considering God's kindness to you (Rom. 11:22). Ask God to clothe you with compassion, kindness, and humility (Col. 3:12).

For Your Family and Friends

Pray for a prevailing spirit of kindness between husbands and wives, parents and children.

For the Church

Pray that your neighborhood may see the kindness, compassion, and forgiveness of God in the way the members of your congregation treat each other and outsiders.

For the Kingdom

Pray that the poor, the mentally ill, the lonely, and the abused may be treated with great kindness and respect in the places where they live and by the people who work to serve them.

For the Unsaved

Pray that you might have an opportunity this week to tell someone of the many kindnesses of the Lord to you (Isa. 63:7).

MARCH 4

Personal Prayer

Praise God, whose incomparable riches are revealed in Christ Jesus (Eph. 2:7). Give thanks for your inheritance that can never perish, spoil, or fade—kept in heaven for you (1 Pet. 1:4). Confess those times when you have valued material things over your inheritance in Jesus Christ. Commit yourself to appreciating daily your inheritance from God (Ps. 16:6). Ask the Holy Spirit to teach you more about what you have received through faith in Christ.

For Your Family and Friends

Pray that parents may be wise enough to pass on a spiritual inheritance to their children—faith in Christ—and to retell the stories of faith from grandparents and older members of the church.

For the Church

Pray that your church's giving may be generous in response to neighborhood needs, knowing that as you give, it will be given you (Lk. 6:38).

For the Kingdom

Pray for the poor who trust in the Lord to meet their needs, that God will be their rich inheritance and their provider.

For the Unsaved

Pray that unsaved persons also may come to share in the inheritance of the saints in the kingdom of light (Col. 1:12).

Prayer Pointer

"Without prayer no work is well done."—ANONYMOUS

MARCH 5

Personal Prayer

Praise God for being the Creator and Lord of the Sabbath. Give thanks for a weekly "day of rest and gladness." Confess any lack of commitment to the holiness of the Christian Sabbath (Ex. 20:8-11). Commit yourself to seeking Jesus' honor in all your Sabbath activities. Ask God to make it a day of true joy and light for you and your loved ones.

For Your Family and Friends

Pray that your loved ones will experience physical and emotional rest from the cares and concerns of daily life.

For the Church

As your church gathers to worship and fellowship, pray that your pastor will be empowered by the Holy Spirit as he brings God's Word to you.

For the Kingdom

Ask God to bring about the day when his people in every nation will "live in peaceful dwelling places . . . in undisturbed places of rest" (Isa. 32:18).

For the Unsaved

Pray that multitudes of unbelievers will hear and obey Jesus' invitation to "come to me, all you who are weary and burdened, and I will give you rest" (Mt. 11:28).

Prayer Pointer

"Prayer is the language of a man burdened with a sense of need." —E. M. Bounds

MARCH 6

Personal Prayer

Praise God, who is majestic in holiness (Ex. 15:11). Give thanks for the privilege of sharing in his holiness (Heb. 12:10). Confess any impure thoughts or actions that remained unconfessed. Commit yourself anew to living the holy life that God has called you to live (1 Thess. 4:7). Ask God to impress upon you the vision of Isaiah: "Holy, holy, holy is the LORD Almighty; the whole earth is full of his glory" (Isa. 6:3).

For Your Family and Friends

Pray that your loved ones will be drawn closer to God as they see your example of holy living.

For the Church

Ask that your church leaders may exhibit holiness as they carry out their responsibilities in your congregation, in their personal lives, and in their work. Pray that their holiness will be based on the holiness of God, rather than on the expectations of others.

For the Kingdom

Holiness in life is mocked by much of our modern culture. Pray that this attribute of God will become an abiding characteristic of his kingdom here on earth.

For the Unsaved

Pray that men and women, boys and girls around the world may turn from sin and seek the Lord—for "without holiness no one will see the Lord" (Heb. 12:14).

MARCH 7

Personal Prayer

Praise God, who fills you with rich spiritual food (Isa. 55:2). Thank God for not allowing you to go hungry for spiritual nourishment. Confess any craving you may have for things which are not spiritually satisfying (55:2). Commit yourself to daily feeding on Jesus, the living bread (Jn. 6:51). Ask God to instill in you a hunger for the Word of Life.

For Your Family and Friends

Pray that any of your loved ones who are physically or spiritually malnourished will receive the food that they need.

For the Church

Pray that those involved in outreach from your congregation will be empowered to offer "the bread of God . . . who comes down from heaven and gives life to the world" (Jn. 6:33).

For the Kingdom

Pray for Christian agencies of mercy who take nourishing food and clean water to starving nations on the African continent. Ask that they may also take the gospel message.

For the Unsaved

Pray for any persons you know who are dying spiritually. Pray for opportunities to invite them to the sumptuous wedding banquet of the king (Mt. 22:2-10).

Prayer Pointer

"Prayerless pews make powerless pulpits." —Anonymous

MARCH 8

Personal Prayer

Praise the Rock—the one whose works are perfect and whose ways are just (Deut. 32:4). Thank him for being the God of truth. Confess any times that you have believed the lies of Satan and acted accordingly. Commit yourself to speaking only the truth in every situation (Eph. 4:25). Ask God to help you be a truthful person in whom he would delight (Ps. 12:2).

For Your Family and Friends

Ask that your loved ones will discover the preciousness of God's truth (Prov. 23:23).

For the Church

Pray that the truth of God's Word will be the solid foundation of the educational programs in your congregation.

For the Kingdom

Reflect on Jn. 8:44. Pray against the influence of Satan—"the father of lies"—as he attempts to subvert the spread of the gospel throughout the earth. Ask that his lies will be exposed in every arena of life.

For the Unsaved

Jesus said, "I am the way and the truth and the life" (Jn. 14:6). Pray that unsaved persons you know will submit themselves to this Savior and begin to live in the light of his teachings.

MARCH 9

Personal Prayer

Praise God for being perfectly just in all his works. Thank him for loving righteousness and justice (Ps. 33:5). Confess any ungodly bias you harbor toward any people. Commit yourself to viewing others with a loving, Christlike attitude. Ask God to help you value justice more highly in all relationships of life.

For Your Family and Friends

Pray that the members of your family will treat each other with mutual love and respect.

For the Church

Ask God to give wisdom and discernment to missionaries in other countries who must suffer injustices and slander for the sake of the gospel. Ask that they will have patience with and love for persons who treat them unfairly.

For the Kingdom

Pray for the uprooting of governments which oppress their citizens and withhold justice from them. Ask that justice will "roll on like a river, righteousness like a never-failing stream" (Amos 5:24) in countries held in the grip of lawlessness.

For the Unsaved

Pray that those who are seeking for God will be drawn to the one who does not show favoritism, but "blesses all who call on him" (Rom. 10:12).

Prayer Pointer

"He who prays as he ought, will endeavor to live as he prays." —John Owen

MARCH 10

Personal Prayer

Praise God for being a welcoming Father. Thank him for preparing an eternal home for all who believe (Jn. 14:2). Confess any unwillingness to show Christian hospitality to others (1 Pet. 4:9). Commit yourself to the practice of hospitality (Rom. 12:13). Ask God to help you separate Christian hospitality from self-absorbed "entertaining."

For Your Family and Friends

Pray for opportunities to use your home or apartment as a tool for ministering the welcoming love of Christ to unsaved loved ones.

For the Church

Pray that the members of your congregation will excel in showing mutual care and intentional acts of love toward each other and to outsiders. Ask God to move your church out of its "comfort zone" when it comes to showing hospitality.

For the Kingdom

Pray that the practice of hospitality might be a significant factor in breaking down walls of misunderstanding and distrust which divide Christians today.

For the Unsaved

Pray that your example of godly, welcoming hospitality might be a first step for some unsaved persons to come to Jesus.

MARCH 11

Personal Prayer

Praise God, the giver of all good gifts (Mt. 7:11). Thank him for the greatest gift of all: his Son, Jesus Christ, our Savior (Lk. 22:19). Confess any lack of thankfulness for all of God's gifts to you. Commit yourself to giving your time, talents, and resources for the gospel. Ask God to grant you a heart of generosity (Lk. 6:38).

For Your Family and Friends

Children and parents are a rich blessing from the Lord. Give thanks for your children, grandchildren, and parents. Pray that your friends, too, will recognize and appreciate the gift of family.

For the Church

Pray that the members of your church will be faithful in managing their personal resources and cheerful in bringing their tithes and offerings to the Lord (2 Cor. 9:7).

For the Kingdom

Pray that all Christian ministries will be blessed with overflowing abundance. Ask God to give wisdom and integrity in the handling of their financial resources.

For the Unsaved

Pray by name for one unsaved friend or loved one. Ask God to open this person's heart to receive the indescribable gift of salvation through faith alone (2 Cor. 9:15; Eph. 2:8-9).

MARCH 12

Personal Prayer

Using Psalm 145, praise the King whose greatness goes beyond your comprehension (145:1, 3). Give thanks for the opportunity to worship him. Confess any unwillingness or negligence in daily worship (145:2). Commit yourself to meditating on his works and proclaiming his great deeds daily (145:3-7). Ask God to lead you in worship that brings him joy.

For Your Family and Friends

Pray for God to open hearts and minds of specific family members to his greatness. Ask God's Spirit to help you tell the stories of his greatness to your children or the children of friends (145:4).

For the Church

Ask God to prompt the saints in your church to join in praising him for his grace, compassion, and patience (145:8-10). Pray that such praise will convince many to follow the Lord (145:11-13).

For the Kingdom

Pray that people around the world will lift their eyes to God (145:13-15). Ask God to show his greatness by continuing to provide for all his creatures (145:16).

For the Unsaved

Ask God to show himself to specific friends in such ways that they are impressed by his great acts of love and call upon him in truth rather than continuing toward destruction (145:17-20). Pray that your faithful praise will attract them to worshipful lives of praise (145:21).

MARCH 13

Personal Prayer

Praise our God, who is unfailing in love and great in compassion (Ps. 51:1-2). Give thanks for the forgiveness of all your past, present, and future sins through Jesus' death 2,000 years ago! Confess that your sin has been against God himself (51:3-5). Commit to the full integrity of having God's truth and wisdom in the inner recesses of your heart (51:6). Ask God for full cleansing, purity, joy, and gladness (51:7-9).

For Your Family and Friends

Pray for a pure and steady heart for each of your household members and friends (51:10). Ask God for a willing spirit to stay in the joy of his Spirit (51:11-12).

For the Church

Pray for the integrity and understanding of your church's leaders. Ask God to give them effectiveness in equipping you to lead people to God's forgiveness and righteousness (51:13-14).

For the Kingdom

Pray that God will raise up religious and political leaders who understand God's desire for right relationships with him rather than mere lip service or token gestures (51:16-17). Ask God to lead his kingdom into true repentance and revival.

For the Unsaved

Pray for God's Spirit to open opportunities for witnessing to a friend. Ask him to lead you and your contacts into a life that brings delight to him (51:18-19).

MARCH 14

Personal Prayer

Read Psalm 24 and praise God as the King of glory, the Lord strong and mighty, the Lord mighty in battle, the Lord almighty! Give thanks for God's power poured into your life and ministries. Confess any attempts to live and minister by your power instead of the power of the Spirit. Commit yourself to being a channel of his powerful love. Ask God to give you clean hands, a pure heart, integrity of soul and honest speech (24:4), so his power can flow through you unhindered.

For Your Family and Friends

Pray that your family and friends will seek God's face (24:3) and be allowed into his presence through Christ. Ask God to work with power on a particular need in your home.

For the Church

Pray that God will powerfully prompt your church to reach out. Ask God to make those outreach efforts effective, bringing many into fellowship with him and his people.

For the Kingdom

Pray that God will strengthen church planters and developers and their core groups. Ask God to make all churches in your denomination effective in their outreach efforts.

For the Unsaved

Pray that God will bring a powerful revival to your nation. Ask him to bring his almighty, King-of-glory presence into your neighborhood through your own example and words.

MARCH 15

Personal Prayer

Read Psalm 139 and praise the all-knowing one who perfectly knows you in every action, thought, and word (139:1, 4). Thank God for the comforting knowledge that he is with you wherever you go (139:5-6). Confess any attempt to flee his all-knowing presence (139:7-12). Commit yourself to learning more about these wonderful human bodies he has made (139:13-16). Ask him to give you a love for knowing his thoughts (139:17-18), an informed hatred for those he hates (139:19-22), and an "open-book" relationship with him (139:23-24).

For Your Family and Friends

Pray that God will give those you know and love a love for knowing him. Ask that they be filled with a conscious desire to think God's thoughts after him (139:17-18).

For the Church

Pray by name for your church's Bible study leaders, Sunday school teachers, and others. Ask God to help them prepare sensitively and thoroughly.

For the Kingdom

Pray that your nation will repent of willful ignorance of God's thoughts and ways. Ask that the beauty and purpose of human life be accepted and promoted (139:12-16).

For the Unsaved

Pray by name for unsaved friends. Ask God to lead you in helping them to truly know him (139:23-24).

MARCH 16

Personal Prayer

Read Psalm 108 and praise the Lord, whose love is higher than the heavens and whose faithfulness reaches to the skies. Give thanks for specific acts of faithfulness to you so far this week. Confess any unfaithfulness which has robbed God of his glory. Commit yourself to praising God among the nations (108:3). Ask him to show you the nations in our cities and around the globe.

For Your Family and Friends

Pray especially for any family members or friends living in another country. Ask God to also use them in showing his glory over all the earth (108:5).

For the Church

Pray for a more visible unity in his church throughout the world, giving the world a credible witness to his love (John 17:20ff). Ask God to focus your eyes more on oneness than differences.

For the Kingdom

Pray that God will be exalted "above the heavens" and have his "glory be over all the earth" (Ps. 108:5) through broadcast missions and on-site missionaries.

For the Unsaved

Pray that everyone will see clearly that human strength cannot win the battle for peoples' hearts (108:12-13). Ask God to gain the victory over spiritual enemies that bind the unsaved.

MARCH 17

Personal Prayer

Praise the Lord, who made and cares for heaven and earth, the sea, and everything in them (Ps. 146:1-6). Give thanks for his personal care for you. Confess instances of putting ultimate trust "in mortal men, who cannot save" (146:3). Commit yourself to putting your hope in the Lord your God. Ask God to help you hand your cares to him through daily prayer.

For Your Family and Friends

Pray that your children (or those of your friends) will learn to present their concerns to God. Ask God to help you authentically model such prayer.

For the Church

Pray that your local church grows as a loving people who genuinely administer God's care. Ask for great wisdom for the deacons and the leaders of care/fellowship committees or groups.

For the Kingdom

Pray that God will continually prompt his people to join him in caring for those oppressed or otherwise in need (146:7-10). Ask God to grant corporate and individual wisdom, persistence, and love in seeking to extend his kingdom.

For the Unsaved

Pray that the witness of God's people will be consistent in word and deed. Ask God to guide you in helping specific people in your neighborhood to put their trust in the caring God.

MARCH 18

Personal Prayer

Praise God as "the Mighty One, God, the Lord" who owns "every animal of the forest . . . the cattle on a thousand hills . . . the creatures of the field . . . the world . . . and all that is in it" (Ps. 50:1, 10-12). Give thanks for the blessings God has put under your care. Confess any irresponsible decisions you have made with his resources. Commit to being a wise and faithful manager of all he gives to you. Ask him to prompt you to wise stewardship from a spirit of thankfulness (50:14-15).

For Your Family and Friends

Pray for God's special treasure of loving relationships. Ask his help in managing these with great care and joy.

For the Church

Pray that your church's members will care for one another in love. Ask God to prompt them to loving generosity with his treasures.

For the Kingdom

Pray for God's blessing on all relief agencies which help people exercise appropriate dominion (Gen. 1:28-30). Ask God to enable you to see and respond to the needs of these aid-givers.

For the Unsaved

Pray that the unsaved will more responsibly care for this planet as they observe the stewardship of God's people.

Prayer Pointer

"Prayer is first and foremost an act of love." —Brennan Manning

MARCH 19

Personal Prayer

Praise the wonderful God who causes mountains and hills to burst into song and all the trees of the fields to clap their hands (Isa. 55:12). Give thanks that the Lord "comforts his people and [has] compassion on his afflicted ones" (Isa. 49:13). Confess any lack of joy which you may have and admit to God your failures to receive his joy. Commit yourself to considering all of life as pure joy, whatever the circumstance, since Jesus Christ is alive and victorious over all. Ask the Lord to restore to you the joy of his salvation (Ps. 51:12), so that you may be a prime exhibit of Christ's life-changing power.

For Your Family and Friends

Pray that your family and friends may have Christian joy. Ask God to help them to discipline themselves in the Christian faith and grow together in genuine love.

For the Church

When your church gathers to worship, ask that members will have a taste of the joyful assembly that is heaven.

For the Kingdom

Pray that relief agencies may operate efficiently and make a lasting difference in the lives of those who are assisted.

For the Unsaved

Ask the Spirit to cause non-Christians whom you know (be specific) to seek out real joy in Jesus.

Prayer Pointer

"Christ actually means prayer to be the great power by which his church should do its work." —Anonymous

MARCH 20

Personal Prayer

Praise the Lord, who is your strength, your rock, your fortress and your deliverer (Ps. 18:1-2). Give thanks that "the weakness of God is stronger than man's strength" (1 Cor. 1:25). Confess your desire to rely upon your own strength. Commit yourself to doing everything through him who gives you strength (Phil. 4:13). Ask God to cause you to serve him with the strength that he provides, so that in all things God may be praised through Jesus Christ (1 Pet. 4:11).

For Your Family and Friends

Ask God to remove habits which destroy and limit relationships among your family and friends, and to replace these with habits which are life-giving and Spirit-led.

For the Church

Pray that your church leaders will be persons of spiritual power and that they will carry "weapons of righteousness" (2 Cor. 6:7) with which to battle the enemy.

For the Kingdom

Ask God to watch over the powerless of the world—the sick, the poor, the orphaned—that his strength would be sufficient to help them endure.

For the Unsaved

The gospel is the power of God for the salvation of everyone who believes (Rom. 1:16). Ask the Lord to apply this power to individuals whom you know are without it.

MARCH 21

Personal Prayer

Praise the One who sits upon his throne, supreme in power and authority. Give thanks that the Almighty is your Father in Jesus Christ. Confess your own hardness of heart and disobedience against God's authority over you. Commit yourself to God so that you "do not let sin reign in your mortal body so that you obey its evil desires" (Rom. 6:12). Ask God to help you endure, so that you may reign with Christ (2 Tim. 2:12).

For Your Family and Friends

Pray that the relationships among your family and friends will be spiritually honest and productive. Pray that Jesus Christ will be a frequent and comfortable topic of conversation.

For the Church

Ask the King of the Church to reveal to your church its opportunities to lead lost persons to Jesus Christ. Pray that church members will be enthusiastic about this task.

For the Kingdom

Pray that ancient hostilities among peoples in various parts of the world will be eased so that life may be spared.

For the Unsaved

At the name of Jesus, every knee will bow and every tongue confess that Jesus Christ is Lord (Phil. 2:10-11). Pray that your unsaved friends will bend their knees to Jesus now and confess him as Lord.

Prayer Pointer

"Prayer moves the hand that moves the world."—John Aikman Wallace

MARCH 22

Personal Prayer

Praise God that he graciously chooses people to belong to him! Give thanks "that in all things God works for the good of those who love him, who have been called according to his purpose" (Rom. 8:28). Confess to the Father any doubts or objections you may have about how he works things out. Commit yourself to the one who chose you in Christ before the creation of the world to be holy and blameless in his sight (Eph. 1:4). Ask that "he who began a good work in you will carry it on to completion until the day of Christ Jesus" (Phil. 1:6).

For Your Family and Friends

Entrust all your loved ones, including all their troubles, to the marvelous care of God. Ask him to work his purpose in their lives.

For the Church

Pray that the educational ministry of the church will lead young and old to dedicate their lives to Jesus Christ.

For the Kingdom

Pray that governmental officials may not be tempted by power or money. Ask God that those who have fallen to these temptations may be changed or removed from their positions.

For the Unsaved

Ask the Holy Spirit to bring new life to particular unsaved persons whom you know. Pray that you may be used in this task.

MARCH 23

Personal Prayer

Praise God that he is the creator of prayer. Give thanks because he gives you an audience with himself whenever you choose to pray. Confess any misuse or neglect of prayer. Commit yourself to making prayer a priority in your life. Ask God to lead you to "approach the throne of grace with confidence, so that [you] may receive mercy and find grace to help [you] in time of need" (Heb. 4:16).

For Your Family and Friends

Ask God to draw your family and friends closer to him and each other through prayer. Pray that their prayers would be "powerful and effective" (Jas. 5:16).

For the Church

Pray that missionaries will be encouraged in their efforts to communicate the good news to those of another culture. Pray that the words will be understandable and relevant.

For the Kingdom

Pray for the rights of Christians to be protected as they speak out for Jesus Christ. Remember especially Christian brothers and sisters who are being severely persecuted for their faith.

For the Unsaved

The Holy Spirit convicts the world of guilt in regard to sin, righteousness, and judgment (Jn. 16:8). Pray that your non-Christian acquaintances will be so convicted, repent, and claim the forgiveness of Jesus Christ.

MARCH 24

Personal Prayer

Praise God because he is the encourager and comforter of his people. Give thanks that God loved you and by his grace gave you eternal encouragement and good hope (2 Thess. 2:16). Ask forgiveness for all those times when fear and anxiety replace the courage that God gives. Commit yourself to seeking God's encouragement to face every obstacle in your life. Ask God to encourage your heart and strengthen you in every good deed and word (2:17).

For Your Family and Friends

Pray that God will help your family and friends to do all their work and play in an excellent, God-glorifying way.

For the Church

Ask God to lead your church to care about welcoming newcomers and including them in the life of the church. Pray that no one be neglected in this important ministry.

For the Kingdom

Pray for special encouragement for teachers as they educate. Pray that parents will be supportive of teachers who seek what is best for students.

For the Unsaved

"There is now no condemnation for those who are in Christ Jesus" (Rom. 8:1). Ask that specific persons whom you know will be free from condemnation as they come to be "in Christ Jesus."

Prayer Pointer

"I have so much to do [today] that I shall spend the first three hours in prayer."
—Martin Luther

MARCH 25

Personal Prayer

Praise God for seeking and saving the lost. Give thanks that Jesus is "the good shepherd [who] lays down his life for the sheep" (Jn. 10:11). Confess those instances and ways in which you ignore the voice of your Shepherd. Commit yourself to learning to be content whatever the circumstances (Phil. 4:11). Ask God to give you the fullness of life which comes with following the Savior.

For Your Family and Friends

Pray that your family and friends will learn to appreciate and respect each other, and that any divisions will be mended.

For the Church

Ask God to teach Christians to ask not "how little?" but rather "how much?" when they make decisions about giving finances. Pray that Christ's great gift of himself will lead Christians to give liberally.

For the Kingdom

Pray for those who serve in law enforcement, that the stress of their jobs will not be too much for them to bear. Ask God to give them special strength to do their jobs well.

For the Unsaved

Pray that non-Christians whom you know will be sensitive to hear the voice of the Good Shepherd and desire to be part of his flock.

MARCH 26

Personal Prayer

Praise God, who is perfect in beauty and holiness (Ps. 50:2). Thank him for making everything beautiful in its time (Eccl. 3:11), including your own life. Confess those times during this past week when your words or actions did not reflect to others the beauty of Christ. Commit yourself to being transformed into his likeness (2 Cor. 3:18). Ask God daily to change the ugliness of sin in your life to his loveliness.

For Your Family and Friends

Pray that your own family will reflect God's beauty in your relationships, so that others may be drawn to God through you.

For the Church

Pray that the spirit of worship may fall upon all who enter your church's sanctuary on Sunday, that they may desire "to gaze upon the beauty of the LORD and to seek him in his temple" (Ps. 27:4).

For the Kingdom

Pray for those in ministry in your denomination, that they may not get so caught up with administrative details that they forget to seek and reflect the Lord's beauty to everyone.

For the Unsaved

Ask God to spread the fragrance of the knowledge of God through you to the people you meet this week (2 Cor. 2:14-16).

MARCH 27

Personal Prayer

Praise Jesus as your King and husband, the bridegroom of the church (Eph. 5:25-27). Give thanks for his power to wash you and make you clean and holy, radiant and without stain or wrinkle. Confess any impure thoughts you may have had this week. Commit yourself to purifying yourself "from everything that contaminates body and spirit, perfecting holiness out of reverence for God" (2 Cor. 7:1). Ask God to help you think about whatever is true, noble, right, pure, lovely, and admirable (Phil. 4:8).

For Your Family and Friends

Pray that the young people you know will not be drawn into sexual relationships outside of marriage. Ask God to give them the grace to resist peer pressure.

For the Church

Pray for pastors who work with couples experiencing marital problems. Ask God to give them the wisdom to counsel effectively and the strength to bear this heavy burden.

For the Kingdom

Pray for sexual purity in all Christian leaders. This is an area where Satan works overtime to discredit the gospel.

For the Unsaved

Ask Jesus to help you invite others to his wedding banquet (Lk. 14:15-23).

Prayer Pointer

"They who have steeped their soul in prayer
Can every anguish calmly bear."—Richard M. Milnes

MARCH 28

Personal Prayer

Express your praise to God as the compassionate Father (Ps. 103:13). Thank him for desiring only good things for his children, including you (Lk. 11:11-13). Confess those times when you have not wanted what God wanted for you or others. Commit yourself to seeking first God's desire—his kingdom and his righteousness (Mt. 6:33). Ask God to "fill you with the knowledge of his will through all spiritual wisdom and understanding" (Col. 1:9).

For Your Family and Friends

Pray that God will give guidance to single persons as they seek to know what God has in store for their future (1 Cor. 7:32-35).

For the Church

Pray that God will place his own desire to reach the lost into the hearts of those who work in your church's outreach ministries. Plead for renewal and a new sense of God's power in evangelism.

For the Kingdom

Pray for Christians living in oppressive conditions, that God's desire for spreading his Word may be so strong in their hearts that they speak the Word boldly, without fear.

For the Unsaved

Pray that your own heart may be set on fire with God's passion to bring all people into his family.

MARCH 29

Personal Prayer

Praise God as the Creator who makes all things new (Rev. 21:5). Give thanks for his power to bring even the most deadened souls to life in Jesus—including your own (Eph. 2:1-5). Confess those times when you have lost faith in God's power to renew and restore. Commit yourself to renewing your mind every day in prayer and in reading God's Word. Ask God to teach you what it means that you are now God's workmanship, created in Christ Jesus to do good works (2:10).

For Your Family and Friends

Pray for marriages that are floundering, that God's power may heal, renew, and restore love and forgiveness to dying relationships.

For the Church

Pray that church education teachers may be effective in renewing the minds of children and adults, so that they may resist conforming to the pattern of this world (Rom. 12:2).

For the Kingdom

Pray that those prayer warriors who intercede daily for politicians and governments around the world will never lose faith in God's power to renew and restore.

For the Unsaved

Pray that those who are outside of God's family may be made new creations in Christ (2 Cor. 5:17).

MARCH 30

Personal Prayer

Give praise to Jesus, the Alpha and the Omega, the First and the Last, the Beginning and the End (Rev. 22:13). Thank him for his promise, "Yes, I am coming soon" (22:12). Confess those periods of time when you have lost sight of the hope of his coming. Commit yourself to waiting each day for "the blessed hope—the glorious appearing of our great God and Savior, Jesus Christ" (Titus 2:13). Ask God to renew in you the hope that "when he appears, we shall be like him, for we shall see him as he is" (1 Jn. 3:2).

For Your Family and Friends

Pray that Christian families may not be consumed with materialism but may long "for a better country—a heavenly one" (Heb. 11:13-16).

For the Church

Pray for world missions, so that "this gospel of the kingdom will be preached in the whole world as a testimony to all nations, and then the end will come" (Mt. 24:14).

For the Kingdom

Pray for social justice agencies in your area, that God's kingdom may be advanced through their work.

For the Unsaved

Ask God to open the eyes of your unsaved friends so that they may see the spiritual kingdom that lies behind the physical realm.

MARCH 31

Personal Prayer

Praise God as Comforter, Immanuel ("God with us"), Paraclete ("one who stands alongside"). Give thanks for his promise: "I . . . have called you in righteousness; I will take hold of your hand" (Isa. 42:6). Confess those times when you have doubted that God's hand has been in front of and behind you, guarding your life (Ps. 139:5). Commit the times of your life into God's hands (Ps. 31:14-15). Ask him to show you how close he is to you.

For Your Family and Friends

Ask God to make his presence known to family members or friends who are going through difficult times (Isa. 43:1-2).

For the Church

Pray that your deacons may be God's hands of compassion and God's presence to those who are struggling, frightened, or lonely.

For the Kingdom

Pray for missionaries who work in Muslim countries, that through them God may "open eyes that are blind, . . . free captives from prison, and . . . release from the dungeon those who sit in darkness" (Isa. 42:7).

For the Unsaved

Ask God to make you his hands of compassion in the life of one unsaved person this week.

Prayer Pointer

"A person must recognize his need for God before he can request divine aid and give God due thanks." —Anonymous

APRIL 1

Personal Prayer

Glorify God as measureless, incomparable, infinite, and generous Giver. Give thanks that his resources are bottomless (Col. 1:15-17). Confess those times when you have not asked for what you have needed, or have asked with the wrong motives (Jas. 4:2-3). Commit yourself to relying on God's resources rather than on your own. Ask God to help you see how rich is the inheritance and how mighty the power that he has given you (Eph. 1:18-19).

For Your Family and Friends

Pray that parents may teach their children how to give cheerfully and generously to God, responding with compassion to needs in the lives of others (2 Cor. 9:7).

For the Church

Pray that church leaders will look beyond apparent financial limitations to claim by faith God's abundant provisions for their ministries (9:8-11).

For the Kingdom

Ask God to provide for the needs of the poor in your area through your own generous giving of time and money.

For the Unsaved

Pray that the church's outpouring of gifts in times of disaster and need may move the unsaved to praise God and commit their lives to him (2 Cor. 9:13).

APRIL 2

Personal Prayer

Praise God for being a great and awesome God (Deut. 7:21). Thank him for bending down low in order to bring salvation and faith to you. Confess times when you've thought God was small and powerless. Commit yourself to worshiping God with "reverence and awe" (Heb. 12:28). Ask for a true sense of awe as you meet God in the sanctuary (Ps. 68:35).

For Your Family and Friends

Pray that the worship experience of your family might be "awesome" because it is centered on an awesome God.

For the Church

Pray that visitors to your church will be struck by the awesomeness of God as they join in worship with you.

For the Kingdom

The psalmist says to God: "How awesome are your deeds! . . . All the earth bows down to you" (Ps. 66:3-4). Pray that God's awesome power might be clearly evident throughout his kingdom worldwide.

For the Unsaved

Ask that the spiritual eyes of the unsaved will be opened so that they will be able to recognize and appreciate God's awesome power and majesty.

Prayer Pointer

"Do not pray by heart, but with the heart."—Anonymous

APRIL 3

Personal Prayer

Praise God for individuals whom he has called to be your spiritual guides. Thank God for establishing order and authority in his church. Confess any lack of appreciation for the responsibility God has given to your pastor, elders, and deacons. Commit yourself to regularly upholding your spiritual leaders in prayer. Ask God to grant you a willingness to follow their leadership.

For Your Family and Friends

Pray that God's design for roles and relationships in your family may be preserved and enhanced. Pray that spiritual leadership in the home may be loving and faithful.

For the Church

Pray by name for your pastor(s), elders, and deacons. "They keep watch over you as men who must give account." Ask that "their work will be a joy, not a burden" (Heb. 13:17).

For the Kingdom

Pray for Christians who serve God in business, government, education, industry, and other fields of labor. Pray that their witness will be clear. Ask that they will not sacrifice spiritual principles as they carry out their tasks for the Lord.

For the Unsaved

Ask God to open the eyes of leaders in your church to the spiritual plight of the unsaved. Pray that they will be active in sharing their faith and so model a lifestyle of evangelism for others to follow.

APRIL 4

Personal Prayer

Praise God, who is light and in whom there is no darkness at all (1 Jn. 1:5). Thank the Lord for being your light and your salvation (Ps. 27:1). Confess any times you have willingly hidden the light of Christ from others. Commit yourself anew to living as a child of the light (Eph. 5:8). Ask—humbly—that you will become increasingly blameless and pure and that God will make you shine like a star in the universe (Phil. 2:15).

For Your Family and Friends

Pray for any family members or friends who are still walking in spiritual darkness. Ask that the light of the world will dawn on them.

For the Church

Pray that the outreach ministries in your church and denomination will drive back spiritual darkness. Pray for a spirit of urgency as real needs are met and lives are changed by the power of Jesus.

For the Kingdom

How big is your vision of the kingdom of God? Share Isaiah's exciting vision: "Nations will come to your light, and kings to the brightness of your dawn" (Isa. 60:3). Ask God to cause "nations" and "kings" to come to Jesus Christ today.

For the Unsaved

Name two or three people who are walking in spiritual darkness. Pray that the Holy Spirit will open their eyes so that they might have the light of life (Jn. 8:12).

APRIL 5

Personal Prayer

Praise God for the wonderful gift of language. Thank him for communicating with you in words and ways which you can understand. Confess those times when you have used words to harm or dishearten another person (Prov. 12:25; 15:1). Commit yourself to keeping your tongue in check at all times (Jas. 3:3-12). Ask God to enable you to overcome the evil which an untamed tongue so quickly breeds in one's life.

For Your Family and Friends

Pray for opportunities to build up and encourage any friends whose spirits may be sagging. Pray that the tongue will be an instrument of peace and not strife in your family life.

For the Church

Uphold those who teach Christian doctrine in your congregation. Pray that they will be careful to teach the truth. Ask that they might communicate spiritual truths in an engaging and effective manner.

For the Kingdom

Pray for ministries and organizations which are translating the Bible into written languages for the first time ever. Ask God to prosper the translation and distribution of his Word.

For the Unsaved

What a wonder that Jesus is the Word made flesh (Jn. 1:1-2, 14). Pray that many who hear of him will repent and believe.

Prayer Pointer

"The more we pray, the more our horizons expand and the more we come to expect from a supernatural, miracle-working God." —Anonymous

APRIL 6

Personal Prayer

Praise God, the one whose name is great among the nations (Mal. 1:11). Give thanks that the good news is being preached in so many countries today and that it has been proclaimed to you, too. Confess anything in your life which hinders your own witness to the saving grace of Christ. Commit yourself to regular prayer support of missionaries whom you know. Ask God to open doors for their ministries.

For Your Family and Friends

Your family can be a missionary family right in your neighborhood! Ask for opportunities for your family to be a witness among your neighbors and friends. (And then be ready when God answers!)

For the Church

Pray for the work of missionaries whom you know in other countries. Ask God to keep them safe from political or religious oppression. Pray that their marriages and family life will be strong.

For the Kingdom

Jesus instructed his followers to "go and make disciples of all nations" (Mt. 28:19). Pray that God will bring about the day when "all nations" have the opportunity to hear and believe the gospel.

For the Unsaved

As you think of unsaved friends, ask God to "open their eyes and turn them from . . . the power of Satan to God, so that they may receive forgiveness of sins and a place among those who are sanctified by faith in [Jesus]" (Acts 26:18).

APRIL 7

Personal Prayer

Praise the Lord for being your shepherd (Psalm 23). Give thanks for those refreshing times when you experience "green pastures" and "quiet waters." Confess any dissatisfaction concerning God's care for you. Commit yourself to faithfully following the Good Shepherd in every area of your life. Ask God to "strengthen and protect you from the evil one" (2 Thess. 3:3).

For Your Family and Friends

Pray that members of your family would have genuine love and concern for each other. Ask especially that your children will reflect Jesus' love as they interact with each other.

For the Church

Pray that your congregation might be known as a loving and caring church. Intercede for those who plan special opportunities for fellowship within the body.

For the Kingdom

Pray for agencies and organizations which provide care in the name of Jesus for the elderly, for those with mental or physical handicaps, and for the ill. Ask God to meet their needs.

For the Unsaved

Ask the Good Shepherd to touch the lives of those who have not yet put their trust in him. Pray that they may experience his loving and redeeming care.

APRIL 8

Personal Prayer

Praise God for the liberality of his love. Give thanks for the ways that he has blessed you. Confess any attempts you have made to meet your needs or the needs of others in your own strength. Commit yourself to a lifestyle of generosity as you handle your personal finances and assets. Ask God to keep your motives pure as you have opportunity to help others (Mt. 6:1).

For Your Family and Friends

Ask God to meet the needs of your family or friends who are experiencing a lack of physical necessities.

For the Church

Pray that the deacons of your church will be persons of integrity and compassion. Intercede for your church treasurer and financial officers as they handle the Lord's finances.

For the Kingdom

Ask God to "throw open the floodgates of heaven and pour out [his] blessing (Mal. 3:10) upon churches, agencies, and organizations which minister in the name of Christ throughout the world.

For the Unsaved

Ask that unsaved persons you know will realize that there is nothing so valuable in all the world as a saving relationship with Jesus Christ. Pray that they will yield to the promptings of the Holy Spirit and give their lives to Christ.

APRIL 9

Personal Prayer

Praise God that he is a provider, meeting "all your needs according to his glorious riches in Christ Jesus" (Phil. 4:19). Thank God that you do not need to believe in luck, chance, fate or fortune. Confess any times in which you have believed in yourself as your provider. Commit yourself to not being "anxious about anything, but in everything, by prayer and petition, with thanksgiving, present your requests to God" (4:6). Ask that God's peace, which transcends all understanding, will guard your heart and mind in Christ Jesus (4:7).

For Your Family and Friends

Ask that those you hold dear will have their minds fixed on whatever is true, noble, right, pure, lovely, admirable, excellent, or praiseworthy (4:8).

For the Church

Ask that God's name will be made great in your private and corporate worship.

For the Kingdom

Pray for those who are suffering from mental illness. Ask that they will find relief and support, and be restored to wholeness.

For the Unsaved

Pray that specific non-Christians whom you know will be struck by the futility of living without God and will seek out a relationship with Jesus Christ.

APRIL 10

Personal Prayer

Adore the merciful God who has given you "new birth into a living hope through the resurrection of Jesus Christ from the dead" (1 Pet. 1:3). Give thanks that you have "an inheritance that can never perish, spoil or fade—kept in heaven for you" (1:4). Seek God's forgiveness as you confess times when you fail to maintain your hope. Commit yourself to seeing trials as opportunities in which your faith "may be proved genuine and may result in praise, glory and honor when Jesus Christ is revealed" (1:7). Ask God to fill you "with an inexpressible and glorious joy" (1:8-9).

For Your Family and Friends

Pray that your family and friends will be given extra patience, wisdom, and strength as they deal with adversities. Ask that these challenges will mature their faith.

For the Church

Pray that your church leaders will be beautiful examples of Christian maturity.

For the Kingdom

Pray that Christians will be diligent stewards of the earth's resources.

For the Unsaved

The Lord says, "Though your sins are like scarlet, they shall be as white as snow" (Isa. 1:18). Pray that unsaved persons will understand that God desires to forgive and that they will seek that forgiveness.

APRIL 11

Personal Prayer

Praise God for his love (1 Jn. 4:16). Give thanks that "we know what love is: Jesus Christ laid down his life for us" (1 Jn. 3:16). Confess those times when you fail to love others. Commit yourself to laying down your life for your brothers and sisters in Christ (3:16). Ask God to drive all fear away with perfect love (1 Jn. 4:18).

For Your Family and Friends

Give thanks to the Father for the family members and friends that he has given you, and ask him to help you love them deeply.

For the Church

Pray that your church will be seen as a valuable asset in your community, and that its love will be so real and apparent that non-Christians will seek it out.

For the Kingdom

Ask God to expose the foolishness and treachery of the kingdom of darkness. Pray that the forces of the kingdom of God, in politics, education, science, media, business, entertainment, church, etc., will be united and focused in their efforts.

For the Unsaved

"God is light; in him there is no darkness at all" (1 Jn. 1:5). Ask God to cause specific non-Christians you know to desire light instead of darkness.

Prayer Pointer

"If we cannot recognize the value of simply being alone with God, without doing anything, we gouge the heart out of Christianity." —Brennan Manning

APRIL 12

Personal Prayer

Praise God for the fact that he has revealed himself to mere mortals. Give thanks that the Lord has spoken plainly about himself and his will in his Word, which is a lamp to your feet and a light for your path (Ps. 119:105). Confess any failures in seeking the teaching, rebuking, correcting, and training in righteousness that come from the inspired Scriptures (2 Tim. 3:16). Commit yourself to being "thoroughly equipped for every good work" (3:17). Ask God to do good works through you.

For Your Family and Friends

Pray that God removes any distractions to wholesome love among your family and friends. Ask that all ungodly priorities and self-interests will be wiped away so that love can abound.

For the Church

Thank God for faithful teachers in the church. Pray that they will be encouraged by the Spirit to communicate life-changing truths.

For the Kingdom

Pray for those nations (name them) in which war has caused great human hardship and many casualties. Ask God to bring peace-loving, stable governments to power in these places.

For the Unsaved

Pray that unsaved persons whom you know will have an interest in studying the Bible, and that they will meet the Author as they do so.

APRIL 13

Personal Prayer

Praise God for being the dwelling place for his saints in all generations (Ps. 90:1). Thank him that before the mountains were born or he had brought forth the earth and the world, from everlasting to everlasting he is God (90:2). Confess your rebellion against God's greatness. Commit yourself to numbering your days rightly, so that you may gain a heart of wisdom (90:12). Ask the Lord to have his favor rest upon you and to establish the work of your hands (90:17).

For Your Family and Friends

Pray that God moves your family and friends to live with dependence upon him and with a wholesome awareness of their own mortality.

For the Church

Pray that the Lord will supply wisdom and perseverance to your church's missionaries (name them) and that they will be blessed with encouraging results in their work.

For the Kingdom

Ask God to give wisdom to those in the justice system who are making decisions about guilt and innocence, that the guilty may be punished properly and the innocent be freed quickly.

For the Unsaved

"Let [the wicked] turn to the LORD, and he will have mercy on him . . ." (Isa. 55:7). Pray that unsaved ones close to you (name them) would turn and seek the mercy of God.

APRIL 14

Personal Prayer

Praise God that he cares about this world. Thank Christ that he calls the church "his" and that he has promised to build it (Mt. 16:18). Confess your own failures in using your time, talents, and tithe as God desires. Commit yourself to being an energetic, ability-using, enthusiastic part of the body in which Christ has placed you. Ask that, as a part of the church, you will live the fact that you belong to all the others (Rom. 12:5).

For Your Family and Friends

Pray that the marriages of your family and friends will be strong, and that spouses will invest time in building and maintaining God-pleasing marriages.

For the Church

Ask God that your congregation will tirelessly live out the love that it has been given in Jesus Christ. Pray that the character and depth of this love will cause non-Christians in your community to want it for themselves.

For the Kingdom

Ask God to cause a woman who is planning the abortion of her baby to change her mind. Pray that abortion clinics will close for lack of business.

For the Unsaved

Ask God to bring you in contact with a non-Christian and allow you the opportunity to tell what God has done for you.

Prayer Pointer

"Prayer is essentially man standing before his God in wonder, awe, and humility; man, made in the image of God, responding to his maker." —George Appleton

APRIL 15

Personal Prayer

Praise God that you know who he is because you have Jesus Christ, "the image of the invisible God" (Col. 1:15). Give thanks that "God was pleased to have all his fullness dwell in [Christ], and through him to reconcile to himself all things . . . by making peace through his blood" (1:19-20). Confess the instances when you spurn the reconciliation that God has accomplished. Commit yourself to continuing in your faith, "established and firm, not moved from the hope held out in the gospel" (1:23). Ask that Christ will have first place in every part of your life, and that nothing else will rival him.

For Your Family and Friends

Pray that those who are wandering away from God will be drawn back, and that they will have a contagious faith.

For the Church

Ask God to change not only what people in your church give, but also how they give. Pray that the uncheerful will become what God loves—cheerful givers (2 Cor. 9:7).

For the Kingdom

As teenagers are bombarded by the lies of "safe sex," ask God to lead them to save their virginity for marriage.

For the Unsaved

Pray that "Christ-less" individuals on your street or in your community will begin to feel a spiritual hunger for the Lord.

APRIL 16

Personal Prayer

Praise the God of Israel, who comes in glory to meet with his people. Thank God for coming to consume the darkness and to make what is purified radiate with his glory (Ezek. 43:1-5). Confess any wickedness that hinders the brightness of his presence. Commit to letting God's glory shine upon you in worship. Ask God to shine through you to others.

For Your Family and Friends

Pray that those close to you will go into God's presence in spirit and in the light of his truth.

For the Church

Pray that, as those at your church look at God's glory, his brightness may be reflected in their faces. Ask God to change them from "glory to glory" (2 Cor. 3:18).

For the Kingdom

Pray that Jesus, the light of the world, will shine through his people and fill the land with the Father's glory. Ask God to mirror his glory to the world through his people.

For the Unsaved

Pray that the Holy Spirit will cause the glory of God to blaze in you, setting your heart on fire for the lost. Ask that God will send forth his Word, bringing his light to lives swamped in darkness.

Prayer Pointer

"Pray not for lighter burdens but for stronger backs." —Theodore Roosevelt

APRIL 17

Personal Prayer

Praise God as your Sovereign Lord (Ezek. 2:5). Give thanks for the true prophets God has placed in your life (2:3). Confess times when you have spent more time critiquing the Lord's spokespersons than listening to his Word through them. Commit to listening to the Word he gives you today. Ask God to help you respond appropriately to what he says.

For Your Family and Friends

Pray that the children have hearts open to God's Word from their earliest years. Ask God to help them keep their ways pure by living according to his Word (Ps. 119:9).

For the Church

Pray that your pastor will present God's message courageously, whether it is accepted or not (Ezek. 2:3-7). Ask God to help all your church's leaders to consistently follow God's Word themselves (2:8).

For the Kingdom

Pray that the civil leaders of your country and community will humbly submit to God's ways. Ask God to use you in clearly and sensitively speaking out to dissuade fellow citizens from evil (3:16-21).

For the Unsaved

Pray to be empowered and emboldened to speak to the unsaved so that you will not be guilty of their blood (3:18-19). Ask God to make your words and lifestyle effective.

APRIL 18

Personal Prayer

Praise God for his world-sized love (Jn. 3:16)! Thank God for loving you before you ever began to love him (Rom. 5:8). Confess times of turning away from the Lord, acknowledging that such betrayal of his love is spiritual prostitution (Ezekiel 16). Commit yourself again to faithfulness in loving God. Ask him to help you live with purity of love toward him.

For Your Family and Friends

Pray that your household will more and more consistently live in God's love. Ask that his love be reflected from your household to your neighborhood.

For the Church

Pray for the Bible studies and other small groups of your church. Ask God to work his kind of intimacy into the lives of each person involved with these groups.

For the Kingdom

Pray that the world will be drawn to Christ through the magnetic love of his church. Ask that the public witness of the church be protected from angry zealots who act with merely human methods.

For the Unsaved

Pray that the purity of your life will draw your contacts from relationships of abuse and despair to the love of God. Ask God's Spirit to convict of sin and convince of righteousness (Jn. 16:8).

Prayer Pointer

"Seven days without prayer makes one weak."—Allen E. Bartlett

APRIL 19

Personal Prayer

Praise God as the all-knowing one. Thank God for caring enough for you to teach you his ways and warn you when you stray. Confess times of willful ignorance of his ways. Commit to listening and following God's directions. Ask him to provide faithful teachers and examples for you.

For Your Family and Friends

Pray that you will be diligent in teaching those under your care. Ask God to help you be an excellent model for your children (or for the children of your friends).

For the Church

Pray that the teachers of the church will be "watchmen" who faithfully relay God's Word to his people (Ezekiel 33). Ask God to prompt them to diligence.

For the Kingdom

Pray that believers will speak boldly to their countrymen about the essential nature of righteous living (Ezek. 33:12-20). Ask God to soften their hearts to hear, repent, and follow him.

For the Unsaved

Thank God that he does not take pleasure in the death of the wicked. Pray for him to work powerfully through you to call people to turn from the foolish ways leading to death to the life-producing ways of his wisdom (33:11).

APRIL 20

Personal Prayer

Praise God as the sovereign Lord (Ezek. 17:22-24) who deserves the praise of all the people-groups of the world! Thank him for making himself known to you. Confess any smallness of your vision of God and his mission in this world. Commit yourself to a world-sized vision. Ask him to show you some specific way to serve him.

For Your Family and Friends

Pray that someone you love will be led by God to be an "on the scene" world missionary. Ask God to thoroughly prepare that person from an early age.

For the Church

Pray that the church will become a "splendid cedar" in which "birds of every kind will nest" (17:23). Ask God to provide through the church an abundance of wisdom, personnel, and financial resources for entering open doors for mission.

For the Kingdom

Pray that the kingdom of the world will soon become the kingdom of our Lord and of his Christ (Rev. 11:15). Ask God to prompt you to pray regularly for his reign to spread.

For the Unsaved

Pray for international students on the campuses of your country. Ask God to reach many of them so that they will go back to their homelands as his ambassadors.

APRIL 21

Personal Prayer

Praise the sovereign Lord who cares for his sheep (Ezek. 34:11). Thank the Lord for shepherding you, caring for you in his rich pasture (34:14). Confess times of wandering away from the side of the Good Shepherd. Commit yourself to rejoicing in the bounty he provides for you. Ask God to help you be a blessing with the blessings you've been given.

For Your Family and Friends

Pray that those closest to you will always remain close to God. Ask God to nurture them to wholeness in his care (34:11-16).

For the Church

Pray that your church's caregiving and fellowship efforts will be led by faithful shepherds who care for the flock (34:1-10). Ask God to give them compassionate diligence to strengthen the weak, heal the sick, and bind up the injured (34:4).

For the Kingdom

Pray that God's covenant of peace will soon be experienced in fullness, when we will fully know that the sovereign Lord is our God and we are his people (34:25-31).

For the Unsaved

Pray that God will search for the lost and bring back the strays, bringing wholeness to them (34:16). Ask him to seek an unsaved or straying friend through you.

APRIL 22

Personal Prayer

Praise God for his powerful actions on your behalf. Thank God for saving you and bringing you into the richness of life with him. Confess attitudes of self-reliance and independence from God. Commit yourself to remembering that all he has placed in your hands is still his. Ask God to give you a giving spirit.

For Your Family and Friends

Pray that children and young Christians will learn patterns of joyful giving early in their walk with God. Ask God to lead them into this joy through your example.

For the Church

Pray that your church's members and regular attendees will be faithful and insightful in giving. Ask that God will open the doors to his ministry resources stored in our bank accounts.

For the Kingdom

Pray that your church will rejoice in its opportunities to be part of spreading God's kingdom throughout the world. Ask God to bring excellent results to the work of relief agencies.

For the Unsaved

Pray that God will show himself holy through his people in the sight of the nations (Ezek. 39:27).

Prayer Pointer

"In the morning, prayer is the key that opens to us the treasures of God's mercies and blessings; in the evening, it is the key that shuts us up under his protection and safeguard." —Anonymous

APRIL 23

Personal Prayer

Praise God for his jealousy toward you (Zech. 8:1-3; Ex. 20:5-6) that roots out rivals for your love or unfaithfulness on your part. Thank God for such love that will not let you go. Confess times at which you have not given God your undivided love and allegiance. Commit yourself to being exclusively devoted to him. Ask God to give you an undivided heart and life for him.

For Your Family and Friends

Pray that your family will willingly demonstrate undivided love for God with open enthusiasm and deep commitment. Ask God to surround your household with an intimate sense of his presence.

For the Church

Pray for your church to be filled with the fires of first-love devotion (Rev. 2:4-5). Ask that your corporate worship will serve to deepen this love.

For the Kingdom

Pray that the Father will convince the world of his love through the unity of Christians with God and one another (Jn. 17:20-23). Ask that barriers to unity be removed.

For the Unsaved

Pray that God's Spirit will convince your neighbors or coworkers that his love is for them. Ask him to use you in the process, showing you specific ways to put love into action.

APRIL 24

Personal Prayer

Praise God, the one mightier than all the officials of all the nations. Give thanks that he is interested in the substance of justice and mercy rather than mere outward forms (Zechariah 7). Confess times during which your walk with God doesn't go much deeper than formality. Commit yourself to a life-style of justice, mercy, and compassion (Zech. 7:9). Ask God to regularly prompt you to loving faithfulness in such a life.

For Your Family and Friends

Pray that your children will develop a sensitivity toward the needs and concerns of others. Ask God to help you model such concern in relationships and contexts where you exercise authority.

For the Church

Pray that your church's leaders will not be sidetracked by mere adherence to forms or accepted patterns. Ask God to fill them with courage to effectively lead you into his justice, mercy, and compassion.

For the Kingdom

Pray that your government officials will adopt God's priorities as their own. Ask God to help them restrain oppression of widows, the fatherless, the aliens, and the poor (7:10).

For the Unsaved

Pray that the practical displays of God-honoring justice, mercy, and compassion will be combined with a clear call to repent and believe. Ask God to draw specific unsaved people you know into his holiness.

APRIL 25

Personal Prayer

Praise God for his great mercy. Thank God for forgiving you and bringing you back after failure and rebellion (Zech. 8:7-8). Confess times of presuming on his patience and mercy. Commit yourself to consistent obedience from a heart of gratitude for God's forgiveness. Ask him to forgive your debts as you have forgiven your debtors, and to lead you not into temptation but to deliver you from evil.

For Your Family and Friends

Pray that your family will forgive one another for past sins, including abuse of any kind. Ask God to bring restoration and wholeness into your household and friendships.

For the Church

Pray that your church will have eyes to see those who need to be brought back into the fold after failure. Ask God's Spirit to convince all to be sensitive and forgiving rather than judgmental and begrudging.

For the Kingdom

Pray that God will inspire you in all relationships and professional involvements to be a peacemaker and restorer. Ask him for the humble courage such work requires.

For the Unsaved

Pray that the unsaved in your network of relationships will be won to the Prince of Peace by seeing fallen Christians restored. Ask God to show them his healing through the mending of your own life.

APRIL 26

Personal Prayer

Praise God as the God of truth. Thank him for replacing the facades of your life with the substantive realities of his truth. Confess any time you've rejected difficult aspects of that truth for the appealing glitter of Satan's lies. Commit yourself to honesty with God, other people, and yourself. Ask God to lead you into fuller and fuller application of his truth to your lifestyle.

For Your Family and Friends

Pray that your children and those of your friends will be taught the truth about God and his world in their schools. Ask God to give special insight to all Christian teachers.

For the Church

Pray for the education departments of your local church and your denomination. Ask him to speak through them so consistently that the church becomes known as the City of Truth (Zech. 8:3).

For the Kingdom

Pray that God's people will speak the truth to each other in all avenues of life, render true and sound judgment in the courts, and keep their word (8:16-17).

For the Unsaved

Pray that such truth-oriented living will break through the lies the Deceiver has used with unsaved neighbors. Ask God to speak his truth in love to one of them through you today.

APRIL 27

Personal Prayer

Praise the Lord Almighty, who allows city dwellers around the world to seek him (Zech. 8:20ff). Thank God for letting you find him. Confess times you have become indifferent and inattentive to his presence. Commit yourself to ongoing communion with him throughout the day. Ask God to regularly fill you with the joy of his salvation (Ps. 51:7-12).

For Your Family and Friends

Pray that God will always be the main guest of your home. Ask him to save each member of your circle of family and friends.

For the Church

Pray for your denomination's mission agency(ies) and any missionaries your church helps to support. Ask God to give you a special way to encourage your missionary(ies) today.

For the Kingdom

Pray that God will move the hearts of national leaders throughout the world to provide open doors for the spread of God's salvation. Ask that the kingdom of this world will become the kingdom of our Lord and of his Christ (Rev. 11:15) very soon!

For the Unsaved

Pray for eyes to see the different groups needing to be evangelized, including groups in cities near you. Ask God to send forth reapers, and to send you to your unsaved acquaintances.

Prayer Pointer

"A vital prayer life in your church leadership is one of the most important indications of your congregation's spiritual life." —Anonymous

APRIL 28

Personal Prayer

Praise God for the fullness of life he brings, from blessings of old age to a community filled with playing boys and girls (Zech. 8:4-5). Give thanks for your own physical and spiritual life. Confess any ways in which you regularly waste moments of your life. Commit yourself to diligent self-control. Ask the Holy Spirit to produce this part of his fruit (Gal. 5:23) in you.

For Your Family and Friends

Pray that the impact of your life will greatly enhance the lives of those close to you. Ask God to help you be consistently pro-life.

For the Church

Pray for your church's deacons and any fellowship-enhancing committee or care-giving groups in your congregation. Ask God to show you specific ways to encourage others.

For the Kingdom

Pray for those agencies showing love in the name of Jesus Christ. Ask God to hold back disasters and other developments which rob people of the fullness of life.

For the Unsaved

Pray for someone you know who is going through especially difficult times without the comfort of God. Ask God to use you in drawing that person to himself.

Prayer Pointer

"O, do not pray for easy lives. Pray to be stronger men. Do not pray for tasks equal to your powers. Pray for powers equal to your tasks." —Phillips Brooks

APRIL 29

Personal Prayer

Praise God, who is the one who can withhold daily necessities or provide for his obedient people (Zech. 8:12-13). Give thanks for abundant crops, necessary moisture, productivity in industry, and other ways in which God provides an abundance of "daily bread." Confess times you have blocked his blessings through disobedience. Commit yourself to trusting and obeying God. Ask God to make you a wide-open channel of his blessings to the world.

For Your Family and Friends

Thank God for daily opportunities to be a blessing in your household. Ask him to give you a generous spirit.

For the Church

Pray that the financial needs of your local church will be abundantly met. Ask God for a devotion that prompts his people to urgently plead for the privilege of sharing (2 Cor. 8:4).

For the Kingdom

Pray that people will be convinced of the folly of living for this world's toys. Ask God to give his people the selfless perspective to seek first God's kingdom and righteousness.

For the Unsaved

Pray that the unsaved around you will see such a difference in your God-honoring values that they will leave materialistic life-styles to take up their cross and follow Jesus. Ask God to continue the fulfillment of his promise to Abraham through you (Gen. 12:2-3).

APRIL 30

Personal Prayer

Praise God for his faithfulness in calling you into fellowship with his Son, Jesus Christ (1 Cor. 1:9). Thank God for the privilege of being his adopted child. Confess those times when you've foolishly acted like an orphan rather than as one of God's own children. Commit yourself to strengthening the fellowship you enjoy with Christ and with other Christians. Ask God to reveal to you anything that might hinder your fellowship with Christ.

For Your Family and Friends

Pray for a close and loving bond to grow between the members of your immediate family. Ask that this bond will be rooted only in Christ Jesus.

For the Church

Ask that the truth of Jesus' promise to be present "where two or three come together in my name" will be very evident in your congregational worship. Pray for the outpouring of God's Spirit in your prayers and praise.

For the Kingdom

Ask God to thwart Satan's efforts to build barriers between Christians, especially believers from differing ethnic backgrounds. Pray for a spirit of love and respect for brothers and sisters of all ethnic backgrounds. Thank God for such a colorful mosaic of believers in his church worldwide!

For the Unsaved

Ask God to draw more and more people from all cultures into his fellowship.